The Role  of Second Language Acquisition

Steve Buckledee

Published 2011 by arima publishing
www.arimapublishing.com

ISBN 978 1 84549 512 1
© Steve Buckledee 2011

All rights reserved

This book is copyright. Subject to statutory exception and to provisions of relevant collective licensing agreements, no part of this publication may be reproduced, stored in a retrieval system, or transmitted in any form or by any means, without the prior written permission of the author.

Printed and bound in the United Kingdom
Typeset in Garamond 12/14

This book is sold subject to the conditions that it shall not, by way of trade or otherwise, be lent, re-sold, hired out, or otherwise circulated without the publisher's prior consent in any form of binding or cover other than that which it is published and without a similar condition including this condition being imposed on the subsequent purchaser.

Abramis is an imprint of arima publishing.

arima publishing
ASK House, Northgate Avenue
Bury St Edmunds, Suffolk IP32 6BB
t: (+44) 01284 700321
www.arimapublishing.com

Contents

Acknowledgements	5
Preface	6-8

1 What is motivation?	**9-25**
1.1 Attitudes vs Motivation	11-13
1.2 Attitudes and language learning	13-17
1.3 Towards a definition of motivation to learn a language	17-20
1.4 Extraordinary language learners: talented, driven or cerebrally traumatised?	21-25

2 Types of motivation and motivation theories	**26-59**
2.1 Gardner's Socio-Educational Model	28-38
2.2 Goal theories	39-40
2.3 Expectancy-value theories	40-41
2.4 Self-determination theory	41-43
2.5 Foraging for knowledge: a neurobiological explanation of motivation	43-45
2.6 Willingness to communicate	46-47
2.7 Task motivation	47-48
2.8 The Cagliari Survey – phase 1	48-59

3 Motivation over time	**60-87**
3.1 Dörnyei and Ottó's Process Model	61-67
3.1.1 The preactional phase	62-64
3.1.2 The actional phase	64-66
3.1.3 The postactional phase	66-67
3.2 Application of the process model	68
3.3 The Cagliari Survey – phase 2	68-80
3.4 The Cagliari Case Study – phase 1	80-87

4 Achievement and attributions	**88-112**
4.1 Weiner's Attribution Theory	89-92
4.2 The Cagliari Survey – phase 3	92-105
4.3 The Cagliari Case Study – phase 2	106-112
5 The Self in L2 motivation	**113-138**
5.1 The personal Self and the social/cultural Self	114-119
5.2 The Cagliari Survey – phase 4	119-129
5.3 The Cagliari Survey – conclusions	130-133
5.4 The Cagliari Case Study – phase 3	133-135
5.5 The Cagliari Case Study – conclusions	136-138
6 The influence of age, gender and learning environment on motivation	**139-158**
6.1 Age, second language acquisition and motivation	140-143
6.2 Gender and L2 motivation	143-148
6.3 The influence of the learning environment	148-158
Afterword	159
Appendix 1	160-162
Appendix 2	163-164
Appendix 3	165-166
Appendix 4	167-168
References	169-175
Index	176-179

Acknowledgements

I would to thank the students of the Faculty of Languages of the University of Cagliari who cooperated with the research project reported in this work. In particular, I am grateful to Marianna Minari and F (name withheld at her own request), who found time in their busy schedules to allow me to interview them.

Preface

Few human endeavours have a failure rate comparable with that of trying to learn a foreign language. A distressingly high number of Britons have no real communicative competence in French although they supposedly studied that language for several years at school, while public schools in the United States appear to be no better at teaching their pupils Spanish. Although the study of Second Language Acquisition (SLA) is a young discipline that has so far generated more questions and hypotheses than definite answers, one of the few things we can say for certain is that there is nothing in either the genes or the drinking water of US and UK citizens to render them incapable of learning an additional language. Similarly, Scandinavians have no biological advantages that predispose them to the successful acquisition of English and German, although visitors to Copenhagen or Stockholm are bound to be impressed by the number of people who can speak one or both of those languages fluently. The fact is that while individuals can be said to have or not have an aptitude for acquiring foreign languages, to talk of entire populations as good or bad language learners is as irrational as any other kind of national stereotyping.

If Danes and Swedes are more successful than Britons or Americans at learning additional languages, a primary reason is that they have greater desire to do so, or, to put it another way, they are more motivated. We all know intuitively what motivation is, but actually defining the term, describing its constituent parts, and adequately explaining the relationship between motivation and achievement is a far from simple matter. What motivation really is, how it can be stimulated and why it strengthens or fades over time are questions that have vexed theorists and practitioners in a wide variety of fields ranging from psychology and the social sciences to education to business and sport. Motivation theories have to account for the beliefs, behaviour and actions of that most complex of organisms, the human being, and it is therefore no surprise to discover that a number of such theories have been proposed and that on occasion competing theories appear to contradict one another.

This book is concerned with the role of motivation in the specific pursuit of trying to learn a second language. It is impossible to neglect more general theories and models of motivation, however, and chapters 1 and 2 address the questions of defining the necessary terminology and describing the various types of motivation that have been identified. Subsequent chapters investigate the maintenance or loss of motivation over time, the causes we attribute to past successes and failures, the notion of the ideal learning self, and how factors such as age, gender, learning styles and learning environment influence motivation.

Chapters 2, 3, 4 and 5 also report the findings of my own research into the motivation of Italian undergraduates studying English at the Faculty of Languages of the University of Cagliari. This work consists of both quantitative research in the form of survey studies, and a more process-oriented approach involving case studies of two students over the duration of their three-year degree course.

It will emerge that while a great deal of important work has been carried out in the field of motivation and SLA, our understanding of this complex relationship is still incomplete. Since far cleverer people than I have not yet come up with all the answers, I make no extravagant claims for this volume's modest contribution to the overall project. I would hope, however, that for someone approaching the subject for the first time, this book might give them some awareness of the issues involved in the highly complicated matter of what makes us want to learn a language in the first place, and, more importantly, what makes us invest enough effort and and exhibit enough staying power to see the task through to a successful conclusion.

1 What is motivation?

Motivation is what gets you started. Habit is what keeps you going.
Jim Rohn

People who are unable to motivate themselves must be content with mediocrity, no matter how impressive their other talents.
Andrew Carnegie

Motivation is when your dreams put on work clothes.
Author unknown

The adjective *motivated* appears in a high percentage of job ads, and will doubtless continue to do so given that the demotivated of this world are unlikely to go to the trouble of making the case that they are victims of discrimination. Self-help books and websites promise us unimaginable success and riches if we learn the secrets of how to motivate ourselves to realise our dreams and ambitions. No one writing on the subject of education would dream of neglecting the question of learners' motivation, why it is sometimes absent and how it can be stimulated. So we can take it as read that even if we struggle to give an adequate definition of motivation, we nevertheless think we know what it is and, what is more, we are convinced that it is fundamental to our achieving success.

In the three quotations that begin this chapter, the link between motivation and achievement is forcefully stated in

Carnegie's affirmation, and in fact it is never difficult to cite examples of highly talented individuals whose lack of drive resulted in their never realising their full potential (we should be wary of such anecdotal evidence, however, since it is equally possible to find cases of people who, without making any great effort, seem to stumble upon success or who have greatness thrust upon them). The anonymous quotation makes the point that having an objective, or a dream, must be allied to effort, while Rohn underlines the need to maintain that effort over time. The complete picture involves knowing what we want to achieve, working hard to make it happen, and persisting with the chosen course.

Similarly, Dörnyei (2001: 8), seeking to identify the recurrent elements in the great number of motivation studies, notes that: 'Perhaps the only thing about motivation most researchers would agree on is that it, by definition, concerns the *direction* and *magnitude* of human behaviour, that is, the *choice* of a particular action, the *persistence* with it, the *effort* expended on it' (Dörnyei's italics).

Skehan (1989: 54) offers the following equation:

Motivation = Effort + Desire to Achieve a Goal + Attitudes

If we take it that for Skehan persistence is subsumed into the broader behavioural characteristic of effort, the significant difference between his definition and Dörnyei's description is the explicit reference to attitudes. Many researchers in the field have explored the relationship of motivation and attitudes – indeed, the most frequently used instrument for measuring motivation and language acquisition is the Attitude/Motivation Test Battery, or AMBT, (Gardner, 1985a) – which immediately raises another question of definitions.

1.1 Attitudes vs Motivation

It is only logical to study motivation and attitudes together since they are to a certain degree overlapping phenomena that determine how a person perceives a situation, a community or an activity; indeed, Gardner, in his Socio-Educational Model of Second Language Learning (1993: 8), indicates motivation and attitudes as two of the six individual variables in the process of acquisition (the other four being intelligence, language aptitude, strategies and language anxiety). Although motivation and attitudes are clearly related, there is, however, an essential difference between them; while the former tends to be unstable, varying in nature and intensity according to mood, recent experience, peer pressure and many other factors, the latter, being a fundamental part of an individual's structure of beliefs and values, are notoriously difficult to modify:

> Attitudes concern evaluative responses to a particular target (e.g., people, institution, situation). They are deeply embedded in the human mind, and are very often not the product of rational deliberation of facts – they can be rooted back in our past or modeled by certain significant people around us. For this reason they are rather pervasive and resistant to change.
>
> (Dörnyei, 2003a: 8,9)

Consequently, while motivation may diminish or strengthen, disappear entirely or mutate into an obsession, attitudes tend to be fixed. This is not to say that they cannot be changed, but it may require a powerful, even revelatory experience to make a person admit that a belief s/he has held for years is actually mistaken.

A second fundamental difference is that the precise nature of someone's motivation is unique to that individual but attitudes, whether positive or negative, may be socially or culturally determined and, as such, can relate to a community rather than a specific person. In the case of language acquisition, a population may harbour an historic grievance against a nation or ethnic group, an attitude that acts as a psychological block on the learning of the language of that community. Scholastic achievement in general is, of course, directly related to pupils' attitudes towards school as an institution and education as a goal, and those attitudes are shaped by a variety of factors, including gender roles, peer group norms and socio-economic class.

Where language learning is concerned, we need to investigate learners' attitudes towards the target language itself – whether they consider it musical, ugly, difficult or easy – and also how they look upon the population(s) most closely associated with that language.

1.2 Attitudes and language learning

For Baker (1988), the five main characteristics of attitudes are:

(i) Attitudes are cognitive (i.e. are capable of being thought about) and affective (have feelings and emotions attached to them).
(ii) Attitudes are dimensional rather than bipolar – they vary in degree of favourability/unfavourability.
(iii) Attitudes predispose a person to act in a certain way, but the relationship between attitudes and actions is not a strong one.
(iv) Attitudes are learnt, not inherited or genetically endowed.
(v) Attitudes tend to persist but they can be modified by experience.

Baker's first two points have implications for the way we conduct research in this field of enquiry: from point (i) we may conclude that the cognitive aspect of attitudes renders them suitable for research and measurement through self-report surveys, and point (ii), their dimensional nature, makes Likert-scale questionnaires an appropriate tool for data collection. Indeed, from Gardner's AMTB, cited above, to the present day, quantitative investigation using questionnaires has been the favoured research method.

Point (iv) underlines the social and cultural origins of attitudes, while Baker's fifth observation allows the hope that even the most entrenched attitudes can be altered. In point (iii) he claims that attitudes are often not translated into actions; however, this assertion does not rule out the possibility of a much stronger link between attitudes and inaction, and in the field of second language acquisition, it is inaction on the part of the learner that results in failure.

The aforementioned failure of many British children to attain even a modest level of communicative ability in French, the language taught in practically all secondary schools in the UK, is often attributed to a question of attitude, specifically the assumption (and presumption) that knowledge of other languages is unnecessary since the rest of the world can speak English. This popular view of British pupils' arrogance allied to idleness is not always backed up by research findings, however. Thornton's 1996 study of 607 14-15 year-olds in Leicestershire found that most did not have negative attitudes towards language learning *per se*, but towards learning the French language in particular. Hostility towards the French language reflected their negative attitudes towards French people; asked to describe the French, the most frequently used adjective was "arrogant". The persistence of such views some five and a half centuries after the end of the Hundred Years' War between England and France attests to both the durability of historic grievances and the success of Britain's culturally retrograde tabloid press in keeping alive negative stereotypes. In contrast, Thornton found that the most frequently used adjective to describe German people was "nice", and many of the pupils surveyed said that they would have preferred to study German, Spanish or Italian (languages which are not available in many schools). This finding confirms that of a previous study conducted by the Linguistic Minorities Project in 1983 (cited by Cook, 2001: 119); asked to list the four major languages of continental Europe according to preference, the order that UK schoolchildren indicated was German, Italian, Spanish, French.

Other cases of negative attitudes towards a nation or people acting as a hindrance to language acquisition include the reluctance of children in some East European countries to learn Russian during the days of the Soviet Union, or native Africans' refusal to acquire active skills in Afrikaans in Apartheid-era South Africa. In contrast, positive attitudes towards a language community, perhaps because of the values associated with it, will facilitate language acquisition, a case in point being the successful learning of English by the same East Europeans who had been unwilling to learn Russian. Language is so closely linked to identity – the preservation of one's own and the rejection of that of the "others" – that difficulty in mutual comprehension may even be encouraged:

> Half a century ago the Northern Indian lingua franca Hindustani (a pidgin that became a Creole) was replaced by Hindi and Urdu. Both of these were originally at least as artificial as Hindustani, yet today, thanks to massive political intervention, they are irrefutably natural languages in their own right and to a large extent mutually incomprehensible.
>
> (Teubert and Cermáková, 2004: 114, 115)

It remains to be seen whether the recent division of what we used to call Serbo-Croat will similarly lead to the development of two distinct languages.

Negative attitudes towards a population and their language are sometimes caused by lack of contact with, and therefore ignorance of, that speech community. Contact Theory (Allport, 1958) postulates that encouraging interpersonal contacts between members of different communities is effective in overcoming harmful stereotypes and prejudice and can foster reciprocal understanding. Dörnyei and Csizér (2005) investigated the case of post-communist Hungary to see how tourism and other international contacts had influenced attitudes towards foreign languages and language learning. They report that: 'The most consistent overall finding in our study was that intercultural contact, by and large, promoted positive intergroup and language attitudes' (p. 351). It is not simply a case of more contact equals better attitudes, however. In the specific case of tourism, the short-term and somewhat superficial nature of the intercultural exchange may actually underscore rather than diminish stereotypes and negative perceptions. This is particularly true when the sheer volume of tourists creates such disruption in the local community that the inconvenience begins to outweigh the economic benefits of hosting foreign holiday-makers.

Very often positive or negative attitudes pervading an entire community will determine an individual's motivation or lack of motivation to learn a certain language. However, as we shall see in chapter 2, there is one type of motivation that may sometimes be strong enough to counteract even very hostile attitudes towards a language community and allow successful aquisition to occur.

1.3 Towards a definition of motivation to learn a language

Motivation is a term that tends to be employed rather loosely, and in the field of L2 acquisition it has 'chiefly been used to refer to long-term stable attitudes in the students' minds' (Cook, 1991: 115), rather than in its true sense as a complex, permeable and therefore changeable phenomenon of which attitudes represent one aspect.

Ellis (2008: 972) offers the general definition that '[…] motivation refers to the effort that learners put into learning an L2 as a result of their need or desire to learn it'. This may be a useful starting point, but an adequate definition clearly requires greater refinement. As we have already noted, Dörnyei (2001: 8) distinguishes between effort and persistence, an important distinction given that language learning is a long-term endeavour involving repeated practice over an extended period. Furthermore, the need to learn a language and the desire to do so are not the same thing, and, as will be explored more fully in the next chapter, need on the one hand and desire on the other may generate different types of motivation, while the presence of both can stimulate the learner in still other ways.

For Gardner (1985b), a motivated individual wants to achieve a certain goal, derives satisfaction from engaging in activities associated with realising that goal, and gains satisfaction from the achievement of the goal. This takes us a step forward since the focus is not merely on the goal and its achievement, but also on the process of striving towards the objective. As regards the specific task of second language acquisition, we may say that the motivated learner is one who does not view the lengthy (and error-strewn) process as a chore to be undertaken reluctantly, but as a challenge to be taken on willingly.

The process that leads an initial desire or need to an end result is evident in the following altogether more comprehensive definition of L2 motivation:

> In a general sense, motivation can be defined as the dynamically changing cumulative arousal in a

person that initiates, directs, coordinates, amplifies, terminates, and evaluates the cognitive and motor processes whereby initial wishes are selected, prioritised, operationalised and (successfully or unsuccesfully) acted out.

(Dörnyei and Ottó, 1998: 65)

In this view of motivation, initial wishes are subject to a conscious process of selecting and prioritising as a prelude to the operational phase of actually endeavouring to bring the wish(es) to fulfilment. Conscious decision-making (directing and coordinating) continues to determine the process of making and sustaining the effort to achieve the goal. Throughout the process, the individual evaluates the progress or lack of progress being made, a key factor in the maintenance, loss or reinforcement of motivation over time. Thus, we appear to have a complete description of the entire process from initial wishes to successful or unsuccessful conclusion.

The process outlined in Dörnyei and Ottó's definition is a conscious one, and in the field of SLA motivation is usually seen as a phenomenon in which the learner is engaged in making conscious choices. Those investigating the same phenomenon from a psychological viewpoint, however, might argue that in language acquistion, as in any other endeavour, an individual's motivation may be at least partially unconscious. As Sorrentino (1996: 640) notes. '[...] thought does not occur in a vacuum; it is often the product of nonconscious forces'. In the specific area of SLA motivation, however, those nonconscious forces have received relatively little attention compared with the rich literature available on motivation theories focusing on the language learner's conscious decisions regarding goals and commitment.

The next chapter will look at some of those theories. It is important to note at the outset, however, that:

> None of the available theories in motivational psychology offers a comprehensive overview of all the critical motivational factors, in the sense that their absence can cancel or significantly weaken any other existing motives, whereas their active presence can boost learning behavior.
> (Dörnyei and Skehan, 2003: 616)

Apart from unconscious motivation, another of the motivational factors not yet accounted for in most theories is that of emotional or affective influences, although in a wider educational context rather than an explicitly SLA-focused approach, Sorrentino et al (2010) have investigated the interplay between cognitive and affective factors. The overall picture, therefore, is of the quest for a truly comprehensive theory of motivation as a work in progress.

1.4 Extraordinary language learners: talented, driven or cerebrally traumatised?

Giuseppe Mezzofanti (1774-1849), an Italian cardinal, spoke thirty-nine languages fluently and was described by Byron as 'a monster of languages, the Briareus of parts of speech, a walking polyglot, and more'. Even Mezzofanti, however, seems linguistically challenged in comparison with Dr Emil Krebs (1867-1930), a German interpreter and translator who could translate from 100 languages and could speak sixty of them. Krebs donated his body to medical research and investigation of his brain showed that his Broca's area, the part of the brain responsible for language acquisition, was organized differently from that of most people. What cannot be known, however, is the extent to which Krebs' extraordinary language learning ability was present from birth or whether the Broca's area of his brain was modified precisely because he spent so much of his time working with foreign languages. The most prominent living "hyperpolyglot"[1] is the Englishman, Donald Kenrick, who speaks seventy languages.

Hyperpolyglottism is an extremely rare phenomenon but "normal" polyglottism is less extraordinary than people living in a largely monolingual culture might imagine. This begs the question of how many languages an individual can

---

[1] A term coined by Prof. Richard Hudson to describe a person who speaks six or more languages fluently.

normally cope with (leaving aside the exceptional cases described above). After conducting a study of polyglots in the Soviet Union, Spivak (1989) proposed "The Law of Seven" since most of the subjects he interviewed declared that they were truly fluent in seven languages, although they often had more limited knowledge of several others. The Law states that most people (note, *most* people) have the capacity to learn between five and nine languages, but seldom more than that. To monolingual adults the very idea of trying to acquire half a dozen additional languages is a terrifying prospect, although there is evidence to suggest that it is the first foreign language that is the most difficult one to learn and that the task becomes less arduous for subsequent languages. This is because learning a second language entails developing effective learning strategies, and those same strategies can later be employed to approach a third or fourth language.

Few would agree with George Bernard Shaw's Professor Higgins, who in *Pygmalion* famously says of his former pupil, Nepommuck: 'He can learn a language in a fortnight – knows dozens of them. A sure mark of a fool.' In reality, the more common reaction in the presence of a polyglot is one of admiration, even awe, since so few of us exploit our potential to acquire up to nine languages, so we wonder at the prodigious achievements of those who do push their language learning ability to the limit. The simple fact is that many people live in an environment in which there is no great need to acquire even one additional language, so they are not motivated to do so.

For a lot of people experience of language learning is limited to studying the compulsory foreign language on the state school syllabus, a task that some pupils (and not necessarily the most intelligent) find relatively painless, even enjoyable, while others (who may excel in other subjects) find extremely frustrating. There is no doubt that certain individuals have a certain aptitude for language acquisition, and researchers who have studied the phenomenon generally agree that aptitude and general intelligence are unrelated (Ellis, 2008: 653). Furthermore, for Gardner and MacIntyre (1992: 215), '[...] in the long run language attitude is probably the single best predictor of achievement in a second language'. For the individual whose language aptitude is not particularly impressive, the deficit has to be compensated by greater effort and persistence, two of the fundamental elements of motivation.

Some individuals are not merely motivated but driven, and their polyglottism derives not from their aptitude, but from an obsession. A well-documented case is that of the American writer, Louis Wolfson (not to be confused with the deceased financier of the same name), a schizophrenic who learnt French, German, Russian and Hebrew as a means to block out English, the native language that he hated. He wrote in French of his struggle[2], but the nature of

---

[2] *Le Schizo et les langues*, Gallimard, 1970.

his illness obviously made it impossible for him to translate the text into his mother tongue. Wolfson's story is clearly an extreme case, but it nevertheless demonstrates that a person not blessed with an exceptional aptitude for language learning can record exceptional language learning achievements.

Just occasionally one hears of a case in which someone acquires a foreign language instantly having made no effort whatsoever. In 2007 Matej Kus, a Czech speedway rider, had an accident during a race and was unconscious for forty-five minutes. When he came to he amazed medical staff by speaking to them in correct, fluent English without a trace of a foreign accent. Before the accident he had only been able to utter a few words of poorly pronounced basic English. For Kus the instantly acquired foreign language did not stick; as he regained his memory of mundane matters, including his name, he completely lost his ability to converse in English. His case, though extremely unusual, is not unique, and it suggests that the human brain has enormous language-learning potential that only a handful of hyperpolyglots manage to exploit to the full. One day it may be possible to activate, deliberately and safely, the instant language function that was accidentally triggered in the brain of Matej Kus, and thus enable us all to acquire as many languages as we need without the frustration and heartache we go through at present. It will not happen tomorrow, and in the meantime cranial trauma is not recommended as a shortcut to language learning. As we await the medical breakthrough, we have no choice but to try to motivate ourselves to learn languages in more traditional ways.

2 Types of motivation and motivation theories

Acquiring a second language is different from learning most other subjects or skills, and not only because of the high failure rate noted in the Preface to this work. The lexicogrammatical norms of a language can be presented to learners in much the same way as the laws of physics or biological taxonomies can be taught, but unlike biology or physics, a language comes with a great deal of cultural baggage attached, which means that actually learning it (as opposed to merely learning *about* it, and not using it for genuine communicative purposes) entails approaching, willingly or reluctantly, a different ethnolinguistic community. Questions of identity are involved, our attitudes toward the target language community play an important role, and successful L2 acquisition implies allowing aspects of an "alien" linguocultural reality to enter the comfort zone of our own culture. It is clear, therefore, that learning a foreign language is not an activity that can be conducted with an air of academic detachment.

Given the social and psychological nature of acquiring a second language, it is perhaps hardly surprising that the first investigations into L2 motivation were grounded not in linguistics but in social psychology, and the methods employed were those of 'a special data-based research tradition in which the various theoretical propositions were explicitly operationalized and empirically tested' (Dörnyei and Skehan, 2003: 613). Work in the field was initiated in Canada by, among others, Robert Gardner, Wallace Lambert, Pat Smythe and Richard Clément, who studied the anglophone and francophone communities of that country and established the rigorous research tradition that prevails to this day in the investigation of L2 motivation investigations (although Dörnyei [2003b: 21-23] notes that the research perspective adopted in motivation study has tended to isolate it from other fields of SLA research). For this reason, this chapter will begin with a look at Gardner's Socio-Educational Model (1985b), which remains highly influential after a quarter of a century.

Broad issues include whether motivation originates within the learner or from an outside source (*intrinsic* vs *extrinsic* motivation), and whether the learner sees the second language as a means to an end (*instrumental* motivation) or as an activity worth pursuing because s/he is in some way attracted to the target language and its speakers (*integrative* motivation). In addition, this chapter presents findings from the first stage of my own research into the L2 motivation of undergraduates at an Italian university.

2.1 Gardner's Socio-Educational Model

It has long been official policy in Canada to encourage the country's anglophone and francophone communities to learn each other's languages and a great deal of time and money has been invested in endeavouring to make the population bilingual. The results have been disappointing: Robert Gardner himself (2001: 11) cites 1996 census figures showing that in five areas of Canada (Newfoundland, Nova Scotia, Saskatchewan, Alberta and British Colombia) more than 90%, of the population speak only English, while in Québec 56% speak only French. In Canada as a whole the figures are 67.07% for English only, 14.30% for French only and 16.97% for both languages. In the late 1950s Gardner and his colleagues began studying the two communities, focusing primarily but by no means exclusively on L1 English speakers attempting to learn L2 French. The first version of the Socio-Educational Model of second language acquisition appeared in 1985, and although it has since been modified as Gardner and others have continued their research, the essential principles have remained unaltered.

The Socio-Educational Model proposes six variables that account for people's relative success or failure in learning a second language in formal educational contexts: intelligence, language aptitude, language learning strategies, language attitudes, motivation and language anxiety. As regards motivation, the model distinguishes between integrative and instrumental motivation:

- *Integrative motivation*: 'motivation to learn a second language because of positive feelings toward the community that speaks that language' (Gardner, 1985b: 82-83). Learners who have integrative motivation wish to interact with the target language community and accept, perhaps welcome, the cultural and psychological implications of such contact.
- *Instrumental motivation*: the wish to learn a second language for utilitarian purposes, such as to get a job or a promotion, to be accepted on a degree course unrelated to languages, or to read scientific papers.

Obviously, the two types of motivation are not mutually exclusive: a person attracted to the Mandarin language and to Chinese culture in general has integrative motivation, but s/he is unlikely to be unaware of the potential advantages of learning Chinese in terms of business opportunities or career advancement, while what starts as instrumental motivation can evolve into greater commitment after positive experiences of contact with L2 speakers. If people have only instrumental motivation, however, the risk is that having acquired the basic competence to carry out certain tasks in the second language, they will not seek to achieve greater proficiency and their L2 will "pidginise" at a relatively elementary level. For this reason, it is integrative motivation that lies at the heart of the Socio-Educational Model.

The model also distinguishes between *motivation* and *orientation*. Many researchers in the field prefer to talk of *goals* rather than orientations – indeed, goal theories of motivation are also dealt with in this chapter – but Gardner has consistently referred to orientations for the phenomena that may trigger motivation but do not in themselves represent motivation. An individual can have integrative or instrumental orientations, or goals, but will not always take the necessary measures to realise those goals. Achievement requires motivation.

For Gardner integrative motivation is composed of three elements: *integrativeness*, *attitudes towards the learning situation* and *motivation*. For the first of these, we will find no better explanation that the one offered by the creator of the model:

> The variable *Integrativeness* reflects a genuine interest in learning the second language in order to come closer to the other language community. At one level, this implies an openness to, and respect for other cultural groups and ways of life. In the extreme, this might involve complete identification with the community (and possibly even withdrawal from one own's original group), but more commonly it might well involve integration within both communities. Since Integrativeness involves emotional identification with another cultural

group, the socio-educational model posits that it will be reflected in an integrative orientation toward learning the second language, a favourable attitude toward the language community, and an openness to other groups in general (i.e., an absence of ethnocentrism).

(Gardner, 2001: 5)

The second element, attitudes towards the learning situation, is concerned with how learners view the language teacher (whether s/he is interesting, boring, competent etc.) and the language course (relevance, nature of the activities and materials, group dynamics within the class etc.). It should be noted that many researchers distinguish between second language *learning* – the conscious study of L2 lexicogrammatical norms, usually involving formal instruction – and *acquisition*, the process of "picking up" a language through interaction with L2 speakers. Gardner and his colleagues in Canada have mostly investigated learning in formal educational contexts.

The third variable, motivation, 'refers to the driving force in any situation' (*Ibid.*: 6). It too consists of three elements: *effort*, *desire to achieve a goal* and *enjoyment of the process of learning*. Integrative motivation can thus be presented as:

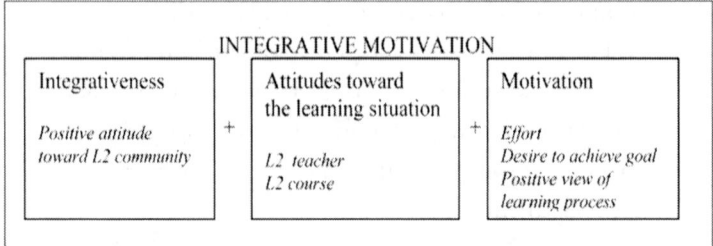

Figure 2.1: integrative motivation

Of the three components that make up Motivation, Gardner (*Ibid.*: 6) notes:

> Each element, by itself, is seen as insufficient to reflect motivation. Some students may display effort, even though they have no strong desire to succeed, and may not find the experience particularly enjoyable. Others may want to learn the language, but may have other things that distract them from their effort. The point is the truly motivated individual displays effort, desire and affect. Motivation is a complex concept.

Other factors may have a positive impact upon motivation, such as instrumental motivation, positive peer pressure or, in the context of school or university, the attainment of high grades or good examination results. Motivation then joins language aptitude and the other four variables noted above in determining the individual's level of achievement in learning the L2.

The idea of integrative motivation that is central to the Socio-Educational Model has stood the test of time. Modifications have been proposed by other researchers and by Gardner himself – Tremblay and Gardner (1995) revised the model to take account of insights from work on goal theories and expectancy-value theories (see below), and Clément, Dörnyei and Noels (1994) revised Gardner's model with the addition of the concept of *linguistic self-confidence* – but few have challenged the essential validity of the construct.

A criticism of Gardner's work is that it is based on the learning of a second language rather than a foreign language. The difference between a second and a foreign language centres on the opportunity to meet and interact with members of the target language community; for anglophone Canadians French is a second language since they have little difficulty in encountering French speakers if they wish to do so, while for Australian schoolchildren French is a foreign language because there is no French-speaking community in their country and a trip to France entails rather more than a short ferry trip. This means that when the target language (TL) is a foreign language, the concept of integrativeness is limited to respect for and indentification with the TL culture and values and does not relate to direct contact with native speakers. That said, modern media in the Global Village permit the truly motivated learner to engage in virtual interaction with people in any country that has the necessary technology, which makes the distinction between second and foreign languages somewhat fuzzy.

Similarly, it has been pointed out that Canadians investigating the learning of French or English are dealing with "big" languages that have international prestige and are frequently adopted as a lingua franca in intercultural exchanges, the implication being that the psychological factors behind motivation to learn a language that does not have the same global role might be different. This is a somewhat specious argument, however, since the importance or usefulness of the target language obviously affects instrumental motivation but there is no logical reason to suppose that the key construct of the Socio-Educational Model, integrative motivation, is any different in the case of "low profile" languages, cultures and populations.

A more convincing challenge to the notion of integrative motivation is based on documented cases of extraordinarily successful learners who pass themselves off as native speakers of the TL and live as apparently normal, well-adjusted citizens in a TL environment, but far from having respect for their host country's values and way of life, actually aim to damage or destroy the society in which they have immersed themselves. Spies and double-agents are often exceptionally proficient L2 users even though they are prepared to risk their lives to undermine the state in which that language is spoken, while in politics and business we find examples of individuals who become fluent in the language of a country or competitor they view with hostility. Oller and Perkins (1978) coined the expression *Machiavellian motivation* for those fairly rare cases of people who learn their enemy's language as part of their plan to manipulate, control or harm those same adversaries. They are exceptions, of course, since in the great majority of cases negative attitudes towards the foreign/second language culture and people impedes language acquisition, so the construct of integrative motivation usually holds good. In the case of the bilingual spy, it might be argued that extraordinarily high instrumental motivation enables an individual to feign a perverse distortion of integrativeness.

To make practical use of the Socio-Educational Model, the Attitude/Motivation Test Battery (AMTB) was devised to assess the non-linguistic goals of a second language programme, 'such aspects as improved understanding of the other community, desire to continue studying the language, an interest in learning other languages, etc.' (Gardner, 1985a: 1). It was a questionnaire using mostly closed-response 7-point Likert scale items in which respondents either circled the answer that best reflected their view or inserted a cross in one of seven spaces to indicate their degree of agreement:

Attitudes toward French Canadians
1. French Canadians are a very sociable, warm-hearted and creative people.

| Strongly Disagree | Moderately Disagree | Slightly Disagree | Neutral | Slightly Agree | Moderately Agree | Strongly Agree |

(*Ibid.*: 17)

My French teacher
efficient ___:___:___:___:___:___:___ inefficient
insensitive ___:___:___:___:___:___:___ sensitive

(*Ibid.*: 24)

Other scales involve a multiple choice format with three possible options:

Motivational Intensity
I actively think about what I have learned in my French class:
a) very frequently.
b) hardly ever.
c) once in awhile.

(*Ibid.*: 20)

The AMTB has been modified over the years, although its key aims and essential nature have remained unaltered. A recent version of it measured five constructs using a total of eleven scales (Gardner, 2001: 8-9):

1. Integrativeness
(i) Integrative orientation (4 items)
(ii) Interest in foreign languages (10 items)
(iii) Attitudes toward French Canadians (10 items)

2. Attitudes toward the learning situation
(iv) Evaluation of the French teacher (10 items)
(v) Evaluation of the French course (10 items)

3. Motivation
(vi) Motivational intensity (10 items)
(vii) Desire to learn French (10 items)
(viii) Attitudes toward learning French (10 items)

4. Instrumental motivation
(ix) Instrumental motivation (4 items)

5. Language anxiety
(x) French class anxiety (10 items)
(xi) French use anxiety (10 items)

Like the Socio-Educational Model, the AMTB has also stood the test of time, and one of the reasons for this is the care taken to ensure that items are appropriately worded and that the questionnaire as a whole meets the required validity and reliability criteria. As noted at the beginning of this chapter, the Canadian researchers who pioneered work in the field of L2 motivation came from a background in social psychology, a discipline that involves frequent use of survey-based research and therefore imposes rigorous standards in questionnaire design and statistical analysis. On occasion linguists also design questionnaires, although not all of them go to the trouble of learning about such arcane matters as construct validity, convergent validity, internal consistency and test-retest reliabilty. Indeed, Dörnyei (2003b: 3) goes as far as to say: '[…] I believe that *most* questionnaires applied in second language (L2) research are somewhat *ad hoc* instruments, and questionnaires with sufficient (and well-documented) psychometric reliability and validity are not that easy to come by in our field' (Dörnyei's italics). Such a charge cannot be levelled at Gardner, whose technical report of the AMTB (1985a) details the measures taken to make the survey as valid and reliable as possible.

Dörnyei and Skehan (2003: 614) note that: 'It is a reflection of the strong theoretical basis of Gardner's work that virtually nobody in the "reform movement" wanted to discard the established findings of the social psychological approach. Rather, most researchers tried to extend the existing paradigms'. As we investigate other motivation theories, we will detect echoes of integrativeness and other constructs of the Socio-Educational Model.

2.2 Goal Theories

Locke and Latham's *goal-setting theory* (1990) posits that human action is prompted by a sense of purpose and for action to take place goals must be set and voluntarily pursued. Types of goal can be distinguished according to *specificity* (the more specific or explicit the goal, the greater the impact on performance), *difficulty* (difficult goals lead to a greater sense of achievement) and *goal commitment* (high commitment requires the individual to see the goal as both important and realistically attainable). Clearly defined goals that are willingly pursued underpin the effort, persistence and choice of appropriate actions required to achieve success.

Another goal theory is that of *goal-orientation* (Pintrich and Schunk, 1996), which evolved from the study of children's behaviour in classroom contexts. The theory distinguishes between *mastery orientation*, which involves striving for mastery of syllabus or textbook content, and *performance orientation*, which is geared towards visible achievement, such as the acquisition of demonstrable skills or getting good grades. Children who exhibit the former have an intrinsic interest in learning and are willing to invest effort and time, while those who display performance orientation are motivated more by the need for public recognition of their ability.

Goal theories have influenced language teaching and, most of all, the design of language teaching materials. Since learning a second language is necessarily a long-term endeavour with the ultimate goal located far into the future, to keep learners focused and motivated it is useful to set a series of subgoals that can be realised within a reasonable time span. For this reason, authors of coursebooks often begin each unit by explicitly listing the new skills students will have acquired by the end of that unit.

2.3 Expectancy-value theories

Expectancy-value theories start from the premise that human beings have an innate desire to learn about the world around them and to acquire skills that will enable them to function better in their environment. Motivation is inherent but it needs to be activated, directed and finetuned to maximise the likelihood of achieving targets. Two key concepts are *expectancy of success* in completing a task and the *value* associated with accomplishing that task. Both factors need to be present if motivation is to be strong and the necessary effort expended to achieve success. If people believe that that a task is simply beyond them, they will not make enough effort and their conviction that they will never achieve a specific goal becomes a self-fulfilling prophecy. In contrast, if they believe that they have a good chance of attaining a goal, they will be motivated to make the required commitment. Similarly, they must believe that the target is worth striving for. A number of expectancy-value theories exist, most notably *self-worth theory* (Covington, 1992) and *self-efficacy theory* (Bandura, 1993). As their names suggest, what they have in common is a focus on learners' views of themselves and their own capabilities.

With relation to second language learning, another researcher based in Canada, Richard Clément (1980), drew on insights from expectancy-value theories, in particular the concept of expectancy of success, in proposing *linguistic self-confidence* as a key factor in successful L2 acquisition. His investigations of English and French speakers in Canada led him to conclude that linguistic self-confidence developed as a consequence of contact with the L2 community since intercultural communication not only encouraged integrativeness, but also improved people's belief in their own ability to learn the language of the other community.

2.4 Self-determination theory

Many theories of motivation distinguish between *intrinsic motivation* (IM, learning or engaging in an activity for its own sake rather than for any utilitarian purpose) and *extrinsic motivation* (EM, learning or doing something as a means to an end or because of an externally imposed obligation). EM bears obvious similarities with instrumental motivation, while 'integrative motivation is similar to IM in that it emphasises positive attitudes toward language learning'

(Noels *et al*, 2003: 54). The two are often seen as being in conflict with extrinsic motivation weakening and possibly destroying intrinsic motivation. An example would be the musically talented youngster who loses enthusiasm if made to have piano lessons and practise scales for hours on end.

Deci and Ryan's *self-determination theory* (1985) refutes the idea that extrinsic motivation is inimical to intrinsic motivation and instead sees the two in their purest forms at opposite ends of a continuum with gradations of external regulation in between. Self-determination is a process of internalising external rewards and encouragement (avoidance of punishment, good grades, parental approval etc.), in effect transforming the external payoff into a boost to intrinsic motivation. It is when the musically gifted child realises that practising those scales has made him/her more able to play the piano for pleasure. The theory also includes *amotivation*, which does not have the negativity of demotivation but indicates lack of both intrinsic and extrinsic regulation.

Factors that favour self-determination in learning contexts are autonomy and a sense of one's own ability, and if one is missing the effect is deleterious; Noels *et al* found that '[…] increased perceptions of freedom of choice and perceived competence are linked to more self-determined forms of behaviour. Conversely, however, low perceptions of freedom of choice and perceived competence are also indicative of higher levels of amotivation' (2003: 53). In other words, a learner who has a sense of her own ability but feels that the teacher exerts excessive control over the learning situation loses motivation. Given this focus on the learner's freedom to choose, it is no coincidence that self-determination theory has influenced SLA research in the area of learner autonomy.

2.5 Foraging for knowledge: a neurobiological explanantion of motivation

Thanks to developments in brain scanning and neuroimaging it is now possible to observe neural activity in some detail. Breakthroughs in our understanding of the mechanisms of the brain led Schumann (2001) to approach the question of learning, and specifically second language learning, from a biological and evolutionary perspective. At the heart of his explanation is the idea that learning is a form of *foraging*:

> In foraging for food, signals indicating reduced glucose levels cause an animal's nervous system to generate an incentive motive to acquire food. That motive is then translated into motor activity whereby the animal moves through its environment in search of food. The desire to acquire certain knowledge or skill similarly constitutes an incentive motive that a learner must translate into activity in order to acquire the desired information or skill. In

other words, a learner must *do* things in order to learn.

(Schumann, 2001: 21 [Schumann's italics])

The urges to forage for food or to forage for mental pabulum are both controlled by dopamine in the neural system, and both instincts require that incentive stimuli be translated into not just cognitive activity, but also motor activity. Learning, then, involves active, goal-directed behaviour. In an earlier work, Schumann (1998) outlined a process in which the learner (or forager) engages in *stimulus appraisal* in which (s)he considers whether the stimuli are novel, pleasant, likely to permit achievement of the goal, within his/her coping potential, and compatible with his/her self- or social image. On the basis of this appraisal, the learner decides whether a learning goal merits sustained effort or not. In the context of the L2 classroom, the appraisal works as follows:

> Let's consider a language class as a foraging patch. The learner will have to locate a "class patch" and will ultimately have to decide how long to remain in that patch. This decision may be influenced by the academic requirements of an educational institution, but let's examine the case in which the learner is acquiring the language without such constraints. The learner will assess the class activities with respect to her perception of the amount of learning achieved for the effort expended. As part of this process, the

learner appraises the activities in the class (i.e., the incentive stimuli) with respect to their novelty, coping challenges, and their impact on her self image. Are they so novel as to be threatening, or are they so routine as to be boring, or are they someplace in between? The learner also has to evaluate whether the level of the class is appropriate to her coping ability. She will also assess the learning activities with respect to their compatibility with her self or social image. Does she find the activities enhancing or diminishing of her self-esteem? We can speculate that these assessments are mediated via dopamine signals which respond to stimuli (activities) which are predictive of reward and which also indicate whether or not such stimuli are worthy of continued attention and effort.

(Schumann, 2001: 25)

The metaphor of foraging presents the learner as an active seeker of knowledge or skills rather than someone who passively absorbs what a teacher chooses to impart. The language learner considers options, makes decisions and adopts strategies, and although a specific learning goal may be abandoned, our general desire for knowledge is as basic as our need to satisfy our hunger.

2.6 Willingness to Communicate

While in L1 willingness to communicate (WTC) is primarily associated with personality traits (shyness, self-esteem etc.), age (the grunting adolescent syndrome) or alcohol consumption, the situation is more complicated in L2 since factors like proficiency, anxiety and linguistic self-confidence come into play. There are some L2 speakers who have a high level of communicative competence yet are reluctant to display their skills, while others who have lower proficiency are happy to chat away and are not unduly distressed if what they say occasionally generates laughter. Some learners are willing to communicate in certain situations but anxiety renders them practically mute in other contexts (and, unfortunately, an examination of oral skills is sometimes one of those contexts).

MacIntyre et al (1998) have considered the multifaceted question of WTC with respect to its linguistic, psychological and social variables, the nature of the learning context, and motivational orientations. They bring together a series of variables under four categories – *social and individual context* (personality and intergroup climate), *affective-cognitive context* (intergroup attitudes, the social situation and communicative competence), *motivational propensities* (interpersonal motivation, intergroup motivation and self-confidence), and *situated antecedents* (desire to communicate with a specific person and state communicative self-confidence) – which interact and together produce a *behavioural intention* (i.e. willingness to communicate) that manifests itself in *communication behaviour* (L2 use).

Because of its multifaceted nature, the WTC construct is a useful tool in examining language learning in educational contexts in which all of the above variables can be readily observed and evaluated.

2.7 Task Motivation

Most language teachers can recall an episode in which a normally keen and well-motivated student showed reluctance to participate in a specific classroom activity or, conversely, an apathetic or even disruptive member of the class engaged in a particular task with uncharacteristic enthusiasm. How learners respond to certain tasks has traditionally been seen in relation to the distinction between *state motivation*, a stable condition, and *trait motivation*, a temporary reaction to a specific situation (Tremblay et al, 1995), with task motivation associated with the latter. Dörnyei (2003b) believes that it is insufficient to subsume task motivation into the broader category of trait motivation and proposes a system comprising three elements: *task execution*, *appraisal* and *action control*. 'While learners are engaged in *executing* a task, they continuously *appraise* the process, and when the ongoing monitoring reveals that progress is slowing, halting or backsliding, they activate the *action control* system to "save" or enhance the action' (*Ibid.*: 16). Not all language teachers would agree with the third stage of this process; for many of us the more common experience is to find that learners who arrive at a negative appraisal of the task respond with inaction, i.e. by ceasing to participate in the classroom activity. However, there is no doubt that the choice of appropriate tasks is a crucial factor in successful L2 learning; indeed, a didactic methodology – *task-based learning* – has emerged (Prabhu, 1987; Willis, 1996), while EFL authors nowadays tend to design activities that will render students active participants (or foragers) in the pursuit of L2 skills rather than passive recipients of the teacher's conveyed wisdom.

2.8 The Cagliari Survey – Phase 1

A feature of Italian universities is the extraordinarily high student drop-out rate in nearly all degree courses (Buckledee, 2008: 160-161). One reason for this is that there is often a lack of continuity between high school and university: students who attended a school whose syllabus is oriented towards the humanities can enrol in science faculties at university, while for modern languages complete beginners are accepted even for languages such as English or French. All universities now require potential students to take a pre-course test, but this usually serves to identify weaknesses that will require remedial action rather than to exclude would-be entrants. As a consequence, it is not unusual for young people to sign up for degree courses for which they are inadequately prepared, a situation that is hardly conducive to literally staying the course. That said, the sheer scale of the drop-out phenomenon – as many as 20% abandon university after just one year (*Ibid.*: 161) – suggests that other forces are at work, and it is not unreasonable to speculate that loss of motivation might be a significant factor. For this reason, a longitudinal, quantitative research project was carried out at the University of Cagliari in Italy to monitor undergraduates studying English at the Faculty of Languages and to investigate developments in their motivation (type and strength, maintenance or loss) over the three years of their degree course. The project was begun in October 2008, when the students had just started their course, and was concluded in June 2011, when those who had not fallen by the wayside and were not *fuori corso* (i.e. still enrolled but not on schedule to graduate within the official three-year duration of the course) sat their final examination in English. A summary of Phase 1 is outlined below. A full report is given in Buckledee (2008).

The subjects of the survey were 150 newly enrolled students who had signed up to do one of the following degree courses: *Lingue e Comunicazione* (Languages and Media Studies), *Lingue e Culture Europee ed Extraeuropee* (Languages and European and Non-European Cultures) and *Lingue per la Mediazione linguistica* (Languages for Linguistic Mediation). For the sake of brevity, the three courses will henceforth be referred to as Lcom, Lcult and Lmed.

All 150 students had opted to study English plus at least one other language from the choice of French, German, Spanish, Arabic, Russian and Japanese. 80.5% were female, which is typical for faculties of modern languages in Italy. 69.33% were in the age range 18-20, and since in Italy there is no tradition of taking a gap-year, most had left school in the summer of 2008. A further 26.66% were aged between 21 and 25 and had presumably had some experience of working, or at least seeking work. Only 4%, six individuals, were 26 or older.

As noted above, the pre-course *verifica* is a diagnostic rather than a selection test and beginners are permitted to enrol, so there was considerable heterogeneity in the subjects' starting level of English. Asked to indicate their current level, 12.08% described their English as elementary, 63.76% opted for pre-intermediate and 24.16% rated their level as intermediate or higher. Given the presence of so many subjects with limited English language skills, it was decided that the questionnaire administered to them should be in Italian. An English version of it is shown in Appendix 1.

The aim of this first phase of the survey was to discover whether these newly enrolled students were primarily driven by intrinsic motivation or instrumental motivation. Two item banks were created to measure the two types of motivation, both of which involved Likert scale items offering six possible responses, the Italian equivalents of: (A) strongly agree; (B) agree; (C) partially agree; (D) partially disagree; (E) disagree; (F) strongly disagree. An even number of response options was chosen to avoid the phenomenon of "sitting on the fence", i.e. when respondents consistently choose the non-committal middle option from an odd number of possibilities. Closed- rather than open-ended response items were used. Although the latter may yield qualitatively richer data, Brown (2001, 37) lists no fewer that nine disadvantages to their employment, particularly relevant drawbacks being that they are more difficult and time-consuming to answer, which often encourages respondents to skip items, while the data generated are difficult for researchers to interpret and analyse. In contrast:

> The major advantage of closed-ended questions is that their coding and tabulation is straightforward and leaves no room for rater subjectivity. Accordingly, these questions are sometimes referred to as 'objective' items. They are particularly suitable for quantitative, statistical analyses because the response options can easily be numerically coded and entered into a computer database.
>
> (Dörnyei 2003a: 35)

A potential difficulty with this research is that I conducted it in the institution where I work, with the consequent risk that respondents would seek to provide the "right" answers

– i.e. the ones they imagined I wanted to see – rather than sincere responses. In an endeavour to counteract this danger, the questionnaire began with a signed statement affirming that the research was an entirely personal initiative, was not commissioned or even encouraged by the university administration, and that the respondents' answers would not have the slightest bearing on the grades they would receive during their degree course. It was stressed that the questionnaires would remain entirely anonymous unless individuals elected to provide the optional datum of their student enrolment number (which would later permit comparison between reported motivation and re-enrolment for the second year of the course). Unsurprisingly, nearly all chose not to give this piece of information and thus preserved their anonymity.

Before the questionnaire was administered to the target subjects it was piloted on a class of 50 freshly enrolled undergraduates studying English language at the other university on the island of Sardinia, the University of Sassari. Analysis of the data produced revealed that responses to one of the items intended to measure intrinsic motivation were in the extremely limited range of two, rather than in the desirable range of five or six. Since all 50 students gave such similar responses, it was clear that the item was practically useless for differentiation purposes and would have to be eliminated from the definitive version of the survey. Similarly, an item was unceremoniously excluded from the instrumental motivation section after the pilot version showed that it had generated answers that bore little correlation with the other items in the section. It was clearly measuring something other than instrumental motivation, and retaining it would have compromised the internal-consistency reliability of that part of the survey. Thus the questionnaire was pared down to the twelve items shown in Appendix 1, six each for intrinsic and instrumental motivation.

The target subjects in Cagliari filled in the questionnaire on 24 October, 2008 while they were attending colleagues' general English lessons (in classes that ran concurrently). The brevity and closed-ended nature of the survey meant that it could be completed in a few minutes, so within half an hour all 150 questionnaires had been filled in and collected (the round figure of precisely 150 was pure chance). I administered the questionnaire personally, which ensured that each class was given precisely the same instructions.

The major findings were as follows:

- Values for intrinsic motivation were much much higher than those for instrumental motivation. 82% of the respondents indicated moderately stronger or considerably stronger intrinsic motivation, broadly similar values for the two types were reported in 14.66% of cases and only 3.33% had moderately or considerably stronger istrumental motivation.

- The variable of age was not particularly significant. The small number of respondents aged 26+ had the highest values for intrinsic motivation but the 18-20 and 21-25 age groups were not that far behind.
- Similarly, gender was not a major distinguishing factor. Of the minority who reported higher instrumental motivation, most were male, and the imbalance in favour of intrinsic motivation was somewhat less pronounced among the males. Even so, 51.72% of the male students indicated considerably higher intrinsic motivation (against 59.17% for the females).
- Starting level was more significant, with those who had indicated their competence in English as intermediate+ reporting notably higher values for intrinsic motivation than the elementary and pre-intermediate students. Indeed, 69.44% of the intermediate+ respondents had considerably higher intrinsic motivation and none at all were at the opposite end of the Likert scale (i.e. considerably higher istrumental motivation).
- By far the most important variable was choice of degree course. 80% of Lmed students reported considerably higher intrinsic motivation while for Lcom and Lcult the figures were 48.57% and 47.62% respectively. A further 14.29% of Lmed students had moderately higher intrinsic motivation, 5.71% had similar values for the two types and none at all reported moderately or considerably higher instrumental motivation.

That most respondents reported generally high motivation was entirely to be expected given that the survey was carried out less than a month into the new academic year when the initial enthusiasm for a new venture had not yet started to fade. Moreover, a degree of self-selection had already occurred in that the students who filled in the questionnaire were those who had shown up for English lessons early in the morning even though attendance on their courses was not obligatory. It might be supposed that even in the first month of the course, those with flimsier motivation had found the option of a lie-in more attractive.

The notable imbalance in favour of intrinsic rather than instrumental motivation can be explained by the fact that these students had chosen to enrol at the Faculty of Languages, and had done so presumably because they had an inherent interest in studying languages in general and the English language in particular. One might expect students of medicine or engineering to have a more pragmatic attitude toward their English course, seeing knowledge of this language as a tool to help them study the discipline that really interests them. The socio-economic context should also be noted; in Sardinia unemployment among young people, graduates included, is high and it is likely that a fair number of the respondents were under no illusion that a degree in modern languages would dramatically improve their job prospects.

In Phase 1 of the survey age and gender appeared to be of little importance in determining degree and type of motivation. The somewhat higher intrinsic motivation among the 26+ age group was possibly due to the fact that some of those respondents had already found employment and were therefore studying English for personal satisfaction rather than to get a job, while the higher instrumental motivation among the male students was possibly indicative of traditional notions of gender roles and the job market. Subsequent phases of the survey were to confirm the minimal influence of these two variables.

As regards starting level, it is hardly surprising that those who have already reached important language-learning goals should be motivated to aim for still higher achievements, for the old adage that success breeds success is often borne out by experience. Indeed, Skehan's *Resultative Motivation Hypothesis* (1989: 49) posits a strong causal link between goal-attainment and willingness to strive for further success.

In considering the influence of choice of degree course, the institutional context must be taken into account: at the Faculty of Languages of the University of Cagliari, of the three degree courses offered Lmed is the one that is most demanding in purely linguistic terms. In addition to the examinations in general English language skills plus more specialized areas of English grammar, phonology and pragmatics that are broadly similar for all three courses, the Lmed syllabus also involves examinations in translation and interpreting. Furthermore, cross-referencing the two variables of degree course and level of competence in English revealed that of the 36 people who rated their skills as intermediate or above, 16 (44.44%) had enrolled on the

Lmed course. In contrast, of those who admitted to having only an elementary level of English, just three had decided to do the Lmed degree. The overall picture, therefore, shows that while the vast majority of the people surveyed have high intrinsic motivation, the highest levels of all are reported by those with the greatest linguistic competence, many of whom opt for the most linguistically challenging course available to them.

The respondents' levels of instrumental motivation were in most cases low in relative rather than absolute terms. Each of items 7-12 on the questionnaire, those intended to measure instrumental motivation, generated the maximum range of responses (six), while the adoption of Brown's procedure (2001: 173-5) to calculate the internal-consistency reliability produced a Cronbach alpha coefficient of 0.66. While this value is not good – for Dörnyei (2001: 204) 'we should aim at reliability coefficients in excess of 0.70' – it is nevertheless within the range of what is acceptable. Consequently, the imbalance between the subjects' intrinsic and instrumental motivations appears to be genuine rather than the result of skewed values produced by serious procedural flaws, so the task is to discover why this situation emerges.

As previously mentioned, the bleak employment prospects for young Sardinians may have led some respondents to make a brutally realistic assessment of what a degree in modern languages could do for them in practical terms. In addition, the timing of the administration of the questionnaire – late October 2008 – also coincided with the worldwide credit crunch and the first indicators of global recession, hardly a moment for humanities undergraduates to feel optimistic about their short-term future. Of the three degree courses, Lmed is the one that ought to have the most direct link with the world of work because of its orientation toward the practical skills of translating and interpreting, yet the students enrolled on this course were those with the strongest imbalance in favour of intrinsic motivation. Despite the usefulness of being able to speak English and/or German on an island heavily dependent upon tourism, the economic climate was such that enrolling on a degree course in modern languages was a matter of personal satisfaction rather then a smart career move. Ideally a language learner would have both intrinsic and instrumental motivation since the specific and clearly defined goals of the latter would complement the enthusiasm generated by the former. However, if the prevailing economic conditions are such that instrumental motivation struggles in barren soil, there is little that a university or its lecturers in modern languages can do to alter the situation.

Of course, there is no reason why intrinsic motivation – if maintained – should not be sufficient to lead to success in second language acquisition. Indeed, as noted in the section on self-determination theory, it has been argued that strong instrumental motivation may sometimes conflict with and eventually undermine intrinsic motivation (i.e. when something that begins as a pleasure mutates first into a duty, then into a chore). Unfortunately, statistics suggest that far from achieving success, a high percentage of the 150 students investigated in phase 1 of this survey will drop out of university without getting a degree. For this reason, the Cagliari survey is a longitudinal study intended to monitor developments over time in the subjects' L2 motivation. The next chapter looks at the temporal dimension of motivation and reports on both phase 2 of the Cagliari survey and phase 1 of a case study also conducted at the University of Cagliari.

3 Motivation over time

In chapter 1 we saw that a principle difference between attitudes and motivation is that the former are resistant to change while the latter undergoes modifications and even quite radical transformations with the passing of time. In this chapter we will consider how and why motivation changes before revisiting our Cagliari students to see whether the enthusiasm displayed in October 2008 was still evident seven or eight months into their degree course.

The temporal dimension is important precisely because second language learning is a long-term activity. As Dörnyei and Skeehan (2003: 617) put it:

> During the lengthy process of mastering certain subject matters, motivation does not remain constant, but is associated with a dynamically changing and evolving mental process, characterized by constant (re)appraisal and balancing of the various internal and external influences that the individual is exposed to. Indeed, even within the duration of a single course of instruction, most learners experience a fluctuation of their enthusiasm/commitment, sometimes on a day-to-day basis.

Those internal and external influences are many and varied: a strengthening or weakening of belief in one's own ability, experiencing success or failure in terms of grades or examination results, receiving either praise or criticism from teachers and/or parents, group dynamics within the class and peer pressure, the distraction of other goals, the nature of classroom tasks, whether opportunities exist to reinforce learning with out-of-class activities, language anxiety, the institutional context (timetable, syllabus etc.) and the teacher's personality and style.

The theories and models described in the previous chapter tend to focus on relatively stable factors such as integrativeness, orientations or self-worth (although the emphasis on ongoing appraisal and evaluation of the learning situation in Schumann's neurobiological approach accounts for the persistence or abandonment of goals), while the long-term nature of language learning cries out for a model that has the temporal dimension at the heart of its theoretical base. Perhaps the most convincing response to those cries has been the *process model* of L2 motivation (Dörnyei and Ottó, 1998; Dörnyei, 2001: 85-100).

3.1 Dörnyei and Ottó's Process Model

This dynamic model identifies three phases in the motivational process: (i) the *preactional stage*, an initial phase in which motivation is generated, goals are set and choices are made; (ii) the *actional phase*, in which the L2 learner responds to the learning situation and conducts an ongoing appraisal of her achievement; (iii) the *postactional stage*, a phase of motivational retrospection that enables the learner to form causal attributions to account for her relative success or failure.

3.1.1 The preactional phase

The preactional phase involves making choices about future action. There are three substages – *goal setting*, *intention formation* and *the initiation of intention enactment* – each of which is subject to a set of motivational influences. The potential language learner begins with wishes, hopes, desires or opportunities that may be influenced by motivational factors with which we are now familiar, such as integrativeness, the prospect of rewards or other instrumental benefits, intrinsic pleasure in the learning process and extrinsic stimuli like parents' expectations or the favourable climate of the language learning environment. In some, though not all cases, those motivational influences will be strong enough to induce the learner to set a goal. The motivational process has now begun.

As we have already seen, having a clearly identified goal is not enough since we often do not take the necessary action to realise our goals. A *goal* is not the same as an *intention*: 'This is an important distinction and it has been made in order to account for the huge difference which exists between the multiple goals and long-term plans the individual may harbour at a given point of time, and the far fewer concrete intentions the individual will hope to carry out' (Dörnyei, 2001: 87). In the second substage, if the process is to continue the goal must harden into a definite intention that entails making a commitment to taking the required action to achieve the chosen goal. Typically, that commitment takes the form of enrolling on a language course intended to take participants to a specified and measurable (by examination) level of L2 competence after a certain number of study hours. Again, the motivational factors at work are not entirely new to us: anticipating success and seeing the goal as important (expectancy-value motivation), believing in one's own ability (self-worth, self-efficacy and linguistic self-confidence), goal orientation (mastery or performance), intrinsic motivation and internalising external rewards or encouragement (self-determination). If the motivational influences are insufficient, the intention will remain precisely that: an intention. If, on the other hand, some or all of those motivational factors are present, the intention is translated into an action plan and the initiation of intention enactment.

In describing this third substage, Dörnyei and Ottó are indebted to Julius Kuhl (1987) and his concept of *action* versus *state orientation*. People in *action orientation mode* are dynamic individuals who visualise themselves engaged in the actions appropriate to their intention. Those in *state orientation mode* focus on the hypothetical or hoped-for outcome of their action rather than the action itself. The relevance to the initiation of intention enactment substage of the process model is that individuals in state orientation mode are apt to dedicate too much time to reflecting upon how to act instead of acting; in other words, the initiation of intention is planned but not truly enacted. Other potential brakes on translating the intention into effective action are allowing oneself to be distracted by competing demands on one's commitment to action or the inability to perceive the consequences of failure to act, both of which are indicative of an insufficiently self-determined individual. At any stage in the process model the impetus to carry on with the L2 learning project may be lost. People who successfully enact the initiation of intention, however, have now crossed over to the actional phase.

3.1.2 *The actional phase*

If the preactional phase involves choice of action, this next phase is concerned with the execution of that action. Three things occur during the actional phase: the learner conducts an ongoing appraisal of the learning process, comparing actual outcomes with those hoped for when the original goal was set and evaluating the nature of the learning experience; given that L2 acquisition is a long-term process, at this stage the learner sets and implements short- or midterm subgoals in the quest for the ultimate goal; on the basis of what her ongoing appraisal informs her, the learner activates self-regulatory or *action control* mechanisms to adjust, reinforce or remedy specific actions within the broad activity of language learning.

As regards ongoing appraisal, Dörnyei and Ottó borrow the five criteria of Schumann's neuobiological model (see section 2.5), i.e. the learning experience is evaluated in terms of its novelty, pleasantness and goal/need significance, whether it is within the learner's coping potential, and how it affects the learner's self- and social image. The learner's degree of self-determination/autonomy (section 2.4) remains a vital factor, as does her appraisal of the aspects of the learning context, such as the nature of classroom tasks, the dynamics of the learning group and the influence of teachers and parents. Essentially, the actional phase requires the learner to weigh up her 'natural tendency to lose sight of goal and get bored/tired of the activity' (Dörnyei, 2001: 98) against her perceptions of what she has achieved so far and what she stands to gain by persevering with the learning project.

In addition to setting subgoals, the learner's action control system commits her to employing certain strategies. These strategies may be directly applicable to the process of L2 learning (e.g. engaging in extracurricular activities such as watching films in the target language), or they may be designed to help her maintain her motivation (e.g. rewarding herself for achieving a good grade).

A conclusion has to be drawn: 'On the basis of the interplay of the appraisal and control processes, the ongoing action will lead to some kind of *actional outcome*: the optimal scenario is that the actor achieves his or her goal, whereas the other extreme is terminating the action completely' (*Ibid.*: 90). Typically, the actional outcome lies somewhere between the optimal scenario and abandonment of the L2 goal, and the learner continues with the action but with modifications either in learning behaviour (adapting present strategies or adopting new ones), or in the goal itself (e.g. downgrading the ambitious goal of L2 fluency to the more realistic and realisable objective of basic communicative competence, which entails returning to the preactional phase). Even if the action is halted, the cessation of the action could be in the nature of an interruption, which implies potential for resumption at a future date, rather than permanent abandonment.

3.1.3 *The postactional phase*

The postactional phase often coincides with an externally programmed cessation of the learning activity, perhaps because the summer holidays have arrived, or because the end-of-term exams are over. 'The main processes during this phase entail evaluating the accomplished action outcome and contemplating inferences to be drawn for future actions' (*Ibid.*: 91). It is a period of critical (or self-critical) retrospection in which the learner considers whether her goal has been achieved, compares actual results with initial aims and hopes, and elaborates *causal attributions* to account for the achievment or non-achievement of objectives (n.b. *attribution theory* will be considered in detail in chapter 4). Having considered why the learning outcome has gone the way it has, the learner then devises her *internal standards* and decides upon future strategies.

Whether the learner elects to suspend or abandon the long-term aim of L2 acquisition, or concludes that it is still within her capabilities, she has to dismiss the original hopes/wishes, goals and intentions and come up with a new set: 'An accomplished intention may clear the way for a subsequent intention leading to a more distant superordinate goal – in this case the postactional motivational process evolves into a preactional phase and the cycle begins anew' (*Ibid.*: 91).

The motivational influences affecting the postactional phase can take the form of positive or negative feedback in the form of examination results and teachers' evaluations, the factors to which the learner attributes her (lack of) success (such attributions are highly subjective and may contradict the evidence of an objective test), and the learner/forager's self-image (again, self-worth, self-efficacy and linguistic self-confidence).

3.2 Application of the process model

The three great virtues of the process model are: (i) more than any other model of motivation, it has the temporal dimension at its theoretical core; (ii) in elaborating their own model, Dörnyei and Ottó succeed in building upon insights from a quarter of a century of work in the field, incorporating such concepts as integrativeness, action/state orientation, self-determination, expectancy-value issues, and the appraisal/self-appraisal mechanisms of the neurobiological approach; (iii) it represents a valuable research tool for the investigation of L2 learners, particularly those studying in a formal educational context. This applicability of the process model to empirical studies, along with its focus on the development of motivation over time, made it a particularly suitable theoretical underpinning for phase 2 of the longitudinal Cagliari Survey.

3.3 The Cagliari Survey – phase 2

Phase 1 of the survey was carried out at the beginning of the academic year when the students had just translated their learning intention into a commitment to action by enrolling on a degree course, purchasing their text books and starting to attend lessons. They had crossed the divide from the preactional phase to the actional phase, but since the questionnaire was administered after very few lessons, the process of ongoing appraisal had barely begun (although from the very first lesson some will have started to form impressions regarding the teacher, the level of the course and their own ability to cope with it). Phase 1 therefore measured initial motivation, and the high values reported reflect the understandable enthusiasm of young people who had just embarked on a new venture.

The phase 2 questionnaire was administered when the students were about to sit their end-of-year written examinations in English in May or June 2009 (they could choose to sit the exam either in May or in June but those who failed it in May could not try again a month later). In this way, 152 people completed the questionnaire (87 in May, 65 in June), compared with 150 who responded to the phase 1 questionnaire at the beginning of the academic year. That an almost identical total number of students completed the two questionnaires is probably a coincidence since it would be reasonable to assume that some who skipped lessons in October nevertheless came to the exam in May or June, and that others who started lessons for some reason opted not to sit the end-of-year exam (given that anonymity was guaranteed in both questionnaires, it is impossible to know how many students only completed one questionnaire). That said, the two samples remain comparable, and the respondents' personal data (age, sex, existing level of English) showed similar patterns in the two administrations.

Ideally, the second questionnaire would have been delayed until the students had completed their end-of-year exams and received the results. At that point they would have been unequivocally in the postactional phase of critical retrospection and attributing causes to past performance. In order to collect data from a high number of respondents, however, this was not an option (in a city on the Mediterranean coast that has a splendid beach and where summer temperatures can rise to 40°C, very few students would have come into the university again after the exams merely to complete a questionnaire). As a consequence, phase 2 of the survey also investigated the learners on the borderline between stages of the process model, in this case between the actional and the postactional phases. Although not an ideal situation, the second questionnaire could nevertheless yield valid data on developments in the learners' motivation over a period of seven or eight months.

An unavoidable problem that was bound to skew the results slightly was the fact that a small percentage of students were exempt from taking the written exam in question because they already possessed external certification of English language skills at the required level (B1 on the Common European Framework). The majority were students of *Lingue per la Mediazione Linguistica*, which meant that the two most significant variables in phase 1 – level of competence in English and opting for the Lmed degree – might be expected to appear less influential in phase 2.

As in phase 1, the questionnaire was worded in Italian to eliminate the risk of distorted feedback resulting from imperfect comprehension of the individual items (the English version is shown in Appendix 2). Item 1 was designed to discover whether the students' overall motivation had increased, remained stable or diminished; the respondents were asked to report on their desire to learn English on a 5-point Likert scale ranging from "greatly increased" to "greatly reduced". Item 2 switched the focus from motivation to achievement; using a similar 5-point scale, the respondents indicated their degree of (dis)satisfaction with their progress in English since the beginning of the academic year. Item 3 was designed to identify factors other than the target language itself to which the students might attribute changes in their motivation, or satisfaction with their achievement to date, or both; the respondents were asked to evaluate on a 5-point scale the teaching of English in the first year of the degree courses, the organization of timetables and syllabi, and the relevance of the chosen degree course to the job market. While in phase 1 an even number of possible responses was offered in order to deny the respondents the opportunity to choose a non-committal central option, in phase 2 a 5-point Likert scale was preferred to discover how many students had substantially unchanged motivation. A summary of the main findings to emerge is given below. A fuller report may be found in Buckledee (2009).

Over the two administrations (May and June 2009) of the questionnaire, all five items yielded the full range of responses from 1 (extremely negative) to 5 (extremely positive). Item 1 asked respondents to indicate how their desire to learn English had changed since the start of the academic year on a Likert scale from 5 to 1 with the options "increased considerably" (5), "increased somewhat" (4), "remained unchanged" (3), "diminished somewhat" (2) and "diminished considerably" (1). The mean Likert scale response was a rather high 3.97. Figures for the five possible responses were as follows:

Table 3.1
Cagliari Survey: Phase 2   Item 1: increase/retention/loss of motivation

Response	Number/Percentage of respondents
increased considerably (5)	42/152 (27.63%) (May 37.93% – June 13.85%)
increased somewhat (4)	71/152 (46.71%) (May 40.23% – June 55.38%)
remained unchanged (3)	34/152 (15.79%) (May 20.69% – June 24.62%)
diminished somewhat (2)	4/152 (2.63%) (May 1.15%% – June 4.62%)
diminished considerably (1)	1/152 (0.66%) (May 0% – June 1.54%)

It is extraordinary that out of 152 respondents, only five admitted to having experienced some degree of loss of desire to learn English while a total of 74.34% reported that their desire to learn the language was either considerably or somewhat increased. After seven or eight months of the degree course, acquisition of L2 English remained very much the goal. As previously noted, however, a goal is not the same thing as motivation, although it is an important component of motivation. Complete motivation also requires sustained effort if a goal is to be achieved.

Item 2 investigated the extent to which the respondents felt they were on course for achieving their goal by inviting them to indicate their degree of satisfaction with the progress they had made in learning English over the preceeding seven or eight months, again on a five point Likert scale with the options "very satisfied" (5), "fairly satisfied" (4), "neither satisfied nor dissatisfied" (3), "somewhat dissatisfied" (2) and "extremely dissatisfied" (1). The mean score on this scale was 3.41 (3.61 for the May respondents, 3.14 for the June respondents) with the following breakdown:

Table 3.2
Cagliari Survey: Phase 2   Item 2: satisfaction with progress made

Response	Number/Percentage of respondents
very satisfied (5)	7/152 (4.61%) (May 8.05% – June 0%)
fairly satisfied (4)	72/152 (47.37%) (May 51.72% – June 41.54%)
neither satisfied nor dissatisfied (3)	56/152 (36.84%) (May 34.49% - June 40.00%
somewhat dissatisfied (2)	10/152 (6.58%) (May 4.60% - June 9.13%)
extremely dissatisfied (1)	7/152 (4.61%) (May 1.15% - June 9.13%)

Only 17 students (11.19%) expressed either moderate or extreme dissatisfaction with the progress they had made, a fact that partially explains the very high values for desire to learn English revealed by item 1. As noted above, in order to ensure a high number of respondents, the questionnaire had to be administered before the students took their end-of-year written examination, and it is quite possible that some of the self-assessments of achievement did not coincide with the objective data subsequently revealed in test results. The anonymity of the questionnaire made it impossible to cross-check.

Many learners, however, are realistic enough to make a fairly accurate assessment of their own ability and/or progress without requiring the confirmation of an examination result, a fact evinced in the divergent responses produced in May and June. Within the institution it has repeatedly been observed that when students can choose to sit an exam in either a first or a second session, the pass-rate is invariably higher in the former. The likely reason for this is that students who know that they are at risk of failing the exam prefer to give themselves as much time as possible to prepare for it, while those who are confident of passing want to get it out of the way. From Table 3.2 we see that of the seven respondents who pronounced themselves very satisfied with their progress, none had elected to take the exam in June, and a notable discrepancy is evident in the figures for those whose self-assessment was one of moderate satisfaction. In contrast, six of the seven students who were extremely dissatisfied with their progress had chosen to maximise their preparation time (or perhaps had merely decided to delay the fateful day), and of those who were somewhat dissatisfied, twice as many took the exam in June as in May. Such behaviour demonstrates that the ongoing appraisal of 'the multitude of stimuli coming from the environment and the progress one has made towards the action outcome' (Dörnyei, 2001: 89) that occurs during the actional phase does indeed lead to action control strategies, in this case an extension of "cramming" time in an attempt to remedy a trend towards an undesirable outcome. When the results of the two exam sessions were known, it emerged that the pessimism of the June candidates had indeed been based on an honest self-appraisal: 66 of the 87 May candidates

(74.5%) passed the exam while the pass rate in June was under 50% (both figures are low because, as noted in the previous chapter, the Faculty allows even complete beginners to enrol on a degree course).

Item 3 sought further data on the respondents' appraisal of the learning situation by asking them to award a mark between 5 (excellent) and 1 (very poor) for three aspects of their English course: the teaching, the organisation of timetables and syllabi, and the relevance of their chosen degree course to the world of work. In the wording of this item the anonymity of the questionnaire was explicitly stated and verbal reassurances were added when the survey was administered. In addition, it was emphasised that the question about teaching concerned the teaching of English only, not other subjects.

Table 3.3

Cagliari Survey: Phase 2   Item 3: learners' ratings of teaching, organisation of timetables and syllabi, and relevance of degree course to the world of work

Item	Mean Likert scale score (max. 5.0)
3a. teaching	3.34 (May 3.46 – June 3.18)
3b. timetables and syllabi	2.84 (May 3.01 – June 2.63)
3c. relevance of degree course	3.46 (May 3.43 – June 3.55)

Appraisals indicating general satisfaction with both the quality of the teaching and the relevance of the degree course add to the overall picture of learners who are apparently still motivated to pursue their goal after seven or eight months in their actional phase. A significant measure of dissatisfaction with the organisation of timetables and syllabi, especially among the June respondents, anticipates a matter investigated in phase 3 of the survey: how learners account for their success or lack of success.

The same variables were checked as in phase 1: age, sex, level of competence in English and choice of degree course. None was statistically significant as regards the responses to item 3, and age and sex had little measurable impact on answers to items 1 and 2. An existing level of English of "intermediate+", which was correlated with higher intrinsic motivation in phase 1, was actually associated with slightly lower desire to learn English in phase 2 (a mean Likert scale score of 3.89, as against 3.97 for all respondents) and had a negligible influence on the respondents' self-assessment of achievement. As previously stated, a small minority of the students with a reasonably high level of English were not among the respondents because they were exempt from the exam that all the others sat. It is difficult to believe, however, that the absence of such a small number of respondents could totally wipe out the trend observed in phase 1.

Once again, choice of degree course was shown to be the most significant variable. Respondents who had chosen

Lmed, the most linguistically demanding course, had the highest level of motivation (or at least, desire to learn English), which confirmed the trend observed in phase 1 (though less emphatically, probably because of the disproportionate number of Lmed students who were exempt from the end-of-year written exam). Lmed students also reported the highest level of satisfaction with their progress to date.

Table 3.4
Cagliari Survey: Phase 2   Item 2: satisfaction with progress made

Degree course	Mean response to item Q1 (desire to learn English)	Mean response to item Q2 (satisfaction with progress)
Lcom	4.11 (May 4.28 – June 3.71)	3.35 (May 3.72 + June 3.00)
Lcult	3.74 (May 3.82 – June 3.61)	3.33 (May 3.32 – June 3.33)
Lmed	4.26 (May 4.44 – June 4.00)	3.61 (May 3.89 – June 3.23)

The overall picture that emerges is one of high levels of desire to learn English, somewhat lower (but only in relative terms) satisfaction with progress made, and appraisals of the learning context that are positive without representing a ringing endorsement. The conditions appear to be present for the retention of motivation.

While noting the apparently high motivation reported by the respondents in this study, we should also take into consideration the fact that the subjects investigated were not a fully representative group of the 2008-09 intake. Before the administration of the questionnaire, a degree of self-selection had already occurred in that the most demotivated students had presumably not even bothered to sit the end-of-year exam. In Italy an average of 20% of undergraduates abandon their degree courses after just one year (Buckledee, 2008: 160), and there is no reason to suppose that the University of Cagliari performs better than other Italian universities in this respect. It would be useful to track down those who quickly decided to quit university, but to do so would be extremely difficult because of a combination of privacy legislation, financial constraints and, most of all, a peculiarity of the Italian university system which makes it difficult to distinguish between a student who has definitely dropped out and one who has merely opted for the slow track to graduation (*Ibid.*:160).

As noted above, a drawback in phase 2 of this survey is the fact that it had to be carried out before the students investigated had received feedback regarding their achievement in the form of examination results. Phase 3 (reported in the next chapter) rectifies that situation and focuses on the attributions learners assign to explain their past performance.

Second language acquisition is a multifaceted, long-term activity and questionnaires featuring closed-ended response items are in some respects a rather blunt instrument for studying such a complex phenomenon. For his reason, it was decided to complement this quantitative approach with research of a qualitative nature in the form of a case study.

3.4 The Cagliari Case Study – phase 1

Students enrolled on the *Lingue e culture* (Lcult) degree course were invited to volunteer to allow me to monitor their progress, attitudes and motivation through a series of structured interviews, and two female learners, M and F, came forward. I approached students on this particular course for the simple reason that I would never have dealings with them in my role as tutor/examiner, so they could express their views without fear of repercussions if their comments were critical of the institution as a whole and the English language department in particular.

Lcult is the most traditional of the language degree courses available in that there is a heavy emphasis on literature, and it tends to be seen as the most suitable degree for students who hope to become language teachers. Students choose two modern languages to study. Although both M and F demonstrated better than average competence in spoken English for first-year students, the structured interviews were conducted in Italian to allow them to choose the words they really wanted to use rather than being limited to the words they knew how to use. The first interview took place on 3 July 2009 when, unlike the respondents who completed the second questionnaire, they knew the outcome of their first-year examination in English. First of all, brief biographical profiles were noted:

- M. Aged 20 and living with her parents in Cagliari. Obtained her high school diploma in the summer of 2008 and enrolled at the Faculty of Languages for 2008-09. Had attended a *liceo scientifico*, i.e. a high school whose syllabus has a scientific orientation. Had also considered enrolling at the Faculty of Medicine but failed the entry test. A full-time student. Languages chosen: English and French.
- F. Aged 22. Not from Cagliari, and therefore living in a hall of residence. High school diploma in 2006 and enrolled at the Faculty of Political Science but left almost immediately when she had the opportunity to travel to Spain. Had attended an *istituto magistrale*, a kind of training college for non-graduate primary school teachers, with a syllabus oriented towards modern languages. Considered herself a full-time student although she worked as a waitress at the weekend. Enrolled at the Faculty of Languages in 2008-09 to study English and German.

It was noted in the previous chapter that in Italy there is not necessarily a link between the type of high school a student attends and his/her subsequent choice of degree course, and this situation is exemplified in M's decision to read modern languages after studying at a scientific high school. Interestingly, she had made an attempt to enrol at the Faculty of Medicine. Also noted in chapter 2 is the fact that "entry" tests in Italian universities generally serve diagnostic purposes and are not used to exclude would-be students. Medicine is an exception in that there is a genuine selection test, and one which the majority of applicants fail. As the interview proceeded, M did not appear particularly regretful about not being accepted as a student of medicine.

F had previously signed up to study political science but had not hesitated to drop out when an attractive alternative presented itself. One of the many reasons that dropping out of a degree course is not a decision that causes great anguish is the fact that most Italian universities have tuition fees that are low by west European standards (furthermore, when this first interview was conducted, the University of Cagliari had the lowest fees in Italy), so abandonment involves neither soul-searching nor great sacrifice. Despite her experience in Spain, F had chosen German rather than Spanish as her second foreign language. This is possibly indicative of instrumental motivation: German tourists are vital to the economy of Sardinia, which makes German a more marketable language than Spanish.

Asked why they had chosen the Lcult degree, M and F indicated precisely the same reasons: (i) personal interest in foreign languages, (ii) love of literature, (iii) their perception of the course as preparation for a career in teaching. Clearly, (i) and (ii) are indicative of intrinsic motivation, and therefore confirm the picture that emerged from phase 1 of the Cagliari survey. The more utilitarian aim represented by (iii) is a little surprising given the context of school closures, falling rolls in the remaining schools and the consequent lack of employment opportunities in state education. Nearly a year into their three-year course, both thought that Lcult had been the right choice.

Their answers were less uniform when it came to identifying the positive and negative aspects of the first ten months of their university experience. M said that she had been pleasantly surprised by the timetable, which had enabled her to attend all her lessons without difficulty. F, in contrast, was critical of the timetable, particularly the lack of a lunch break, and she also felt that too many lessons were conducted in traditional classrooms while the language labs stood empty. M's main criticism was that for some subjects (though not English) there was insufficient advanced notice of exam dates, which made it difficult for students to prepare adequately. On the positive side, F cited the *tutorati*, a system in which the Faculty's better graduates conduct supplementary lessons with first-year students.

While noting M and F's different observations of what is good and not so good about the learning context, in both cases one is struck by the practical nature of the aspects cited: lessons, classrooms vs language labs, timetable, examination dates. What emerged during this interview was that in an institution in which attendance is not compulsory (indeed, many students are never seen between one exam session and the next), both M and F were making every effort to participate actively in the learning process by getting to class (including supplementary lessons) and were engaged in an ongoing appraisal that included criticism of factors that could impede their goal-achievment (exam dates, failure to use language labs). In terms of Dórnyei and Ottó's process model, they were demonstrating behaviour typical of learners who had emerged from the preactional phase committed to action, and in the actional phase were involved in assessing the learning situation in order to implement strategies aimed at enabling them to stay on course for goal attainment.

They were then asked the hypothetical question: "If you were the dean of this Faculty, what changes would you make?" Both said that they would establish stronger links between the Faculty of Languages and the university's Language Centre. The Language Centre provides courses and tests for faculties that do not have their own language teachers, provides Italian lessons for Erasmus exchange students and also has courses to which the general public can sign up. It is also an examination centre for the internationally recognised TEFL iBT English language test. For reasons that need not be explained in the present work, the Language Centre is much better resourced than the Faculty of Languages, has state-of-the-art equipment and smaller class sizes. In short, for students whose motivational influences include a sense of autonomy and the ability to implement self-regulatory strategies, exploiting the opportunities offered by the Language Centre represents positive action to remedy perceived shortcomings in the learning situation within the Faculty.

That shortcomings exist is evinced in M's observation that if she were dean she would appoint more staff to teach languages, a perceptive appraisal given that the staff-student ratio in Italian universities is embarrassing for a G7 country. Excessively large English language classes in the Faculty of Languages is a factor that can inhibit goal attainment, although for learners whose action control mechanisms are functioning well, the solution is simply to turn to another structure within the university. Many learners ignore this readily available opportunity; M and F clearly did not.

A second hypothetical question asked them what they would do if they were head of the English language department. F said she would change the syllabus to place greater emphasis on the culture of anglophone societies, which suggests that she is influenced by integrative motivation. M's focus was on tasks as she suggested that English should become the language of instruction for other disciplines taught in the Faculty.

Asked if they intended to take advantage of the opportunity to spend some months abroad as part of the EU's Erasmus student exchange programme, F said that she hoped to be able to go either to Germany or to the UK. M did not rule out the possibility but thought she probably would not apply for an exchange.

Finally, when questioned about whether they intended to re-enrol for the second year of the course, both answered with an emphatic yes.

Throughout the interview both students spoke with enthusiasm and displayed a real commitment to achieving their goals. They appeared to share many characteristics: both enjoyed language learning for its own sake (intrinsic motivation), their shared love of L2 literature and F's declared interest in L2 culture suggested integrative motivation, both demonstrated discernment in their ongoing appraisal of the learning situation and self-determination in adopting appropriate strategies to help them remain focused on working towards their target.

At face value the similarities between M and F's learning behaviour are not unusual. In an educational context it is perfectly natural for two students who share the same approach to their task to gravitate towards each other, establish a friendship, and then if one volunteers to cooperate with a researcher, the other is likely to follow suit. However, the similarities revealed in this first interview suddenly appear a good deal less normal and predictable when we consider another key influence on motivation, that of achievement.

In the English language examinations at the Faculty of Languages in Cagliari students first all sit a written test of general English, which is awarded a numerical mark out of 30 with 18/30 being the minimum pass mark. Those who pass the written test then take an oral examination that consists partly of an evaluation of their general communicative skills, but is primarily an assessment of their understanding of a more theoretical area of language study, such as pragmatics or discourse analysis. Their final mark, again out of 30, reflects their performance in both the written and oral parts of the examination. In 2009 things went very well for M: she passed the written test with a score of 27/30, then must have performed exceptionally well in the oral for she received a final mark of 30/30. F failed the written test with 15/30 and therefore was not admitted to the oral.

Despite this disappointment, during this interview F did not give the slightest indication that she had ever considered abandoning her language-learning goal. Her underlying belief in her own ability (self-worth) appeared to be intact, as did her confidence that she would find a way to realise her goal (linguistic self-confidence). Clearly an autonomous learner, at this stage F's enthusiasm for the task was still a match for that of the altogether more successful M. She still had the distraction of examinations in other subjects, however, and it was tempting to hypothesise that once she really stopped for the summer and entered the postactional phase, the deeper reflection upon her own performance and the formation of causal attributions that occurs during that period of retrospection might dampen her enthusiasm somewhat.

The very different achievements of M and F suggested that the next stage of the Cagliari case study, like the third phase of the Cagliari survey, should focus on how learners account for their past performance.

4 Achievement and attributions

In the context of SLA, attributions are the reasons we offer to explain our past successes or failures in learning the target language. These reasons are subjective and, as Dörnyei (2005: 79) notes, they 'considerably shape our motivational disposition underlying future action'. As noted in the preceding chapter, assigning causal attributions to past performance is fundamental to the postactional phase of the process model, and the nature of those attributions is a key factor in whether the learner sets new goals and begins the learning cycle once again.

The two most obvious attributions are ability and effort, and according to Attribution Theory assigning past failure to lack of ability – i.e. to a permanent condition over which the individual has no control – will greatly inhibit future strivings, while confessing to lack of effort – a temporary shortcoming that can be rectified – will have a much less deleterious effect on subsequent attempts to achieve success. If the aim is acquisition of an L2, the individual who declares that she is just not cut out for language learning has erected a psychological barrier that she is unlikely to overcome, while the classmate who admits that she did not study sufficiently before her exam has left the door wide open to success in the re-sit following expenditure of rather more effort. It is important, however, to distinguish between lack of effort on a specific occasion and the same phenomenon as habitual behaviour, the former being eminently controllable and the latter considerably less so.

Given that language learning is an activity that frequently results in failure and abandonment, it is perhaps surprising that the effect of attributions has not been studied more. Dörnyei (2001: 57) believes that this is partly due to the tradition of using quantitative research methods to investigate L2 motivation: '[…] the effects of causal attributions are complex, varying as a function of the type of attributions made and the attributional style and biases of the learners, and questionnaire-based studies focusing on linear relationships of broad categories have not been adequate to do this intricate process justice'. Later in this chapter the findings of both the quantitative Cagliari survey and the qualitative Cagliari case study are reported.

4.1 Weiner's Attribution Theory

For Bernard Weiner (1986, 1992) the key factors to consider in explaining learning achievement or non-achievement are whether the causes are internal or external to the learner, whether they are stable or unstable, and whether the learner can exert some degree of control over them. For example:

INTERNAL/stable/*uncontrollable*, e.g. ability, aptitude
INTERNAL/stable/*controllable*, e.g. typical effort
INTERNAL/unstable/*uncontrollable*, e.g. mood, health
INTERNAL/unstable/*controllable*, e.g. effort on a specific occasion
EXTERNAL/stable/*uncontrollable*, e.g. conditions imposed by school
EXTERNAL/stable/*controllable*, e.g. teacher's bias
EXTERNAL/unstable/*uncontrollable*, e.g. luck
EXTERNAL/unstable/*controllable*, e.g. (lack of) help from friends

If learners remain highly motivated despite disappointing results we may hypothesise that they maintain a positive self-concept and an underlying faith in their own ability (as in the case of F in the Cagliari case study). This would imply that they attribute past failure either to external causes, thus exonerating themselves from personal responsibility, or to internal causes that are unstable and uncontrollable, such as anxiety or a bad mood, which do not represent an impediment to future success (bad moods pass, anxiety sometimes fades with time and experience). Empirical research supports this hypothesis. Ushioda (2003), in her study of Irish learners of French, discovered that those who maintained a positive view of themselves as language learners attributed past success to stable, internal causes such as their own ability and habitual willingness to work hard, and attributed past failure either to external causes, such as the lack of opportunity to interact with French speakers, or to unstable internal causes, typically a short-term lack of effort.

As stated above, attributions are subjective, and as such are the product of the individual's perspective. To examine the question of perspective, Williams *et al* (2001) conducted research in a secondary school in Bahrain that involved asking not just the students to attribute causes for their relative success or failure in learning English, but also invited their teachers to give reasons for their pupils' performance. To account for past failure, the two attributions most frequently cited by the students were inadequate teaching methods and lack of support from family and teachers (*Ibid.*: 180), that is two external causes. Success was most commonly attributed to willingness to practise (*Ibid.*: 178), an internal cause that is both stable and controllable. Their teachers saw things from a rather different perspective. To explain past failure the top three attributions were inadequate teaching materials (presumably a higher authority, such as a ministry, imposed those materials), the students' insufficient knowledge of the basics of English, and the students' personality (*Ibid.*: 179), all, from the teachers' point of view, external causes. To account for success, the second attribution was teaching methods, over which the teacher has total control, which came just behind, paradoxically, teaching materials (*Ibid.*: 177).

The former vice-president of the United States, Hubert H. Humphrey, once said: 'To err is human. To blame it on someone else is politics.' Today politicians are said to "put a spin" on past events to divert responsibility for failure (attributing it to an external cause) and appropriate credit for success (claiming an internal cause), and they thoroughly deserve our contempt for doing so. It is not necessarily a bad thing, however, if language learners adopt a highly partial approach when accounting for their own performance since a little self-delusion may help them to preserve a positive self-concept and thus maintain their motivation with respect to future learning behaviour. Phase 3 of the Cagliari survey was conceived with the purpose of investigating the relations between motivation, success or failure, and the attribution of causes for past performance.

4.2 The Cagliari Survey – phase 3

The question of when to administer the third questionnaire presented the same dilemma as that encountered in phase 2: since students skip lessons but not exams, the best way to ensure a high number of respondents was to conduct the survey when they were about to sit their 2nd year English language written exams in June (again in two sessions, one on the 3rd and the other on the 22nd). A further advantage was that abundant staff were on hand to help supervise, thus ensuring that the questionnaires were completed quickly and without consultations with friends. The same disadvantage was present, i.e. that the respondents were asked to assess their own performance before receiving the results of the end-of-year examination. This time, however, it was possible to make a very broad distinction between successful and unsuccessful learners: the 70 "successful" learners were those who were due to take the 2nd year exam, and had therefore kept pace with course requirements, while the 30 "unsuccessful" learners were those who had to re-sit the 1st year exam that they should have passed twelve months earlier. The inverted commas serve to signal the fact that in many cases those who were still on track were only successful in relative terms, while some of those who had to repeat the 1st year exams were not necessarily unsuccessful by their own estimation. Some who had passed the 1st year exam may nevertheless have been disappointed by the grades achieved; similarly, since, as previously noted, the Faculty allows complete beginners to enrol, it is possible that some who had started from zero were pleased with their progress despite not having passed the first exam yet.

A total of 100 respondents completed this third questionnaire, compared with 152 for the phase 2 survey in May/June 2009 and 150 who had filled in the first questionnaire in October 2008. That a third of the subjects of the 2008-09 intake had apparently fallen by the wayside in just twenty months is testament to the high drop-out rate that suggested the need for this research project in the first place. The neat round figures – 100 respondents, 70 "successful" and 30 "unsuccessful" learners – were entirely coincidental.

Once again, the questionnaire was in Italian (an English version is given in Appendix 3), and it contained just three items. As in phase 2, items 1 and 2 focussed on desire to learn English and satisfaction with progress respectively. Item 1 asked respondents to report on their desire to learn English on a 5-point Likert scale ranging from "greatly increased" to "greatly reduced". Item 2 presented a 6-point Likert scale (an even number of possible responses to avoid non-committal answers) and invited respondents to indicate their level of satisfaction with their progress in English, responses A-C signalling various degrees of satisfaction and D-F different levels of dissatisfaction. Those who answered A-C were then directed to a third item that required them to account for their relative success by indicating one of three given causes and/or writing a brief open-ended response. The D-F respondents were asked to explain their relative failure, again from three given causes plus the option of inserting their own attribution. As in phases 1 and 2, the questionnaire was anonymous and the only personal data required were designed to check the variables of age, gender, starting level of English and choice of degree course.

It should be noted that phase 3 of this project coincided with extraordinary circumstances, which could not possibly have been predicted when this work began in 2008, that were likely to skew slightly any investigation of university students' motivation in Italy. At the time students and lecturers throughout the country were highly concerned about a highly controversial proposal (now passed into law) to reform the university system. Indeed, many in Cagliari and throughout the country had been actively protesting. Every effort was therefore made to emphasise the fact that in the first two items of the questionnaire the students were being asked to give information about the specific activity of learning the English language – their desire to do so and their assessment of their own performance – and not about their experience of university in a more general sense. That said, the third item, the matter of attributions, obviously extended to the institutional and learning context.

As regards the broad distinction between successful and unsuccessful learners and the variables of age, starting level and choice of degree course (gender was found to be statistically irrelevant), the main findings are given below. A full report may be found in Buckledee (in press).

- The younger students were more likely to be successful. Among "successful" learners, 74.62% were in the age range 19-21, against 55.17% of "unsuccessful" learners. 6.69% of the "unsuccessful" learners were in the 27+ age range, against 1.49% of the "successful" learners.
- Unsurprisingly, there was a high correlation between starting level and success measured by examination passes. 31.03% of "unsuccessful" students indicated that their English had been elementary at the time of enrolment, while 27.69% of "successful" learners indicated a starting level of intermediate+.

- Choice of degree course was once again a significant factor with Lmed students having the lowest representation in percentage terms among the "unsuccessful" learners and the highest representation among the "successful" learners. In contrast with the phase 1 results, however, the difference between Lmed and the other degree courses was not emphatic.
- As regards item 1, values for desire to learn English were higher among "successful" than "unsuccessful" learners but not greatly so (mean Likert scale responses of 3.76 and 3.31 respectively [max. 5.0]). Interestingly, "successful" Lmed students reported the lowest value (3.46) while "successful" Lcult students reported a surge in desire to learn English (4.25).
- For item 2 a similar pattern emerged. "Successful" learners indicated only moderately greater satisfaction with progress made than "unsuccessful" learners (mean Likert scale responses of 3.84 and 3.38 respectively [max. 6.0]. Among the "successful" learners, Lmed students were the least satisfied (3.58) and Lcult students the most satisfied (4.19).

It is difficult to account for the age factor without conducting qualitative research. It is possible, however, that some of the older respondents had a history of poor performance, perhaps having to repeat a year at high school or, not an unusual practice in Italy, having already started and abandoned another degree course in a different Faculty.

In otherwise wholly predictable results for the variable of starting level, one figure stood out: out of thirty "unsuccessful" learners, two indicated intermediate+ as their level of English when they had enrolled. This is extraordinary in that those two students had failed the pre-intermediate level 1st year exam, and had possibly failed two re-sits. Interesting questions of attribution are raised when an institution's assessment of a learner is so obviously at odds with that learner's self-assessment.

Although the Lmed students remained measurably the most successful, in comparison with phases 1 and 2 their lead over the Lcom and Lcult students was found to be greatly reduced. This fact may well be related to the relatively low values for desire to learn English and satisfaction with progress reported by "successful" Lmed students. Without conducting interviews, we can only speculate as to why learners who began in October 2008 with very high intrinsic motivation and, in many cases, a good starting level (phase 1) had apparently lost enthusiasm, although a tempting conjecture is that those with the highest expectations at the beginning of the degree course were bound to be the first to suffer disillusionment if things did not run as smoothly as hoped. It should be noted that these unexpected responses to items 1 and 2 came from those Lmed students who had passed their 1st year exam, so it is not unreasonable to assume that by June 2010 people who had set themselves particularly high standards felt that they had fallen short of their personal targets despite having achieved the goals set by the educational institution.

Similarly, the raw figures tell us nothing about the apparent increase in desire to learn English and satisfaction with progress reported by the Lcult students, who had the lowest values on both scale in phase 2. There may be a very simple explanation, such as different English teachers in the first and second years, but again we cannot know without interviewing the learners.

What is surprising is that for items 1 and 2 the gulf between the two groups is not wider given that the "unsuccessful" learners had had three earlier opportunities to pass the exam they were going to take yet again after completing the questionnaire. Of the 30 unsuccessful learners, ten declared themselves "more satisfied than dissatisfied" with their progress in English, three opted for "satisfied" and one even indicated that she was "very satisfied". The apparent paradox of 14 out of 30 respondents describing themselves as satisfied with their progress despite repeated failure in examinations should be seen in the light of the earlier datum concerning starting level. 31% began the degree course with only elementary L2 skills, so it is conceivable that some felt that they had made reasonable progress in English despite not yet reaching the competence required to pass the exam.

Neither had the experience of failure had a devastating effect upon the learners' desire to learn English. Only one signalled "greatly reduced" desire, eight went for "somewhat reduced", seven said their desire was unchanged, eight indicated "somewhat increased" and six had retained their motivation to such an extent that they described their desire to learn English as "greatly increased". These figures will be considered below with reference to the data for attributions.

Table 4.1 deals with those learners who were dissatisfied with their progress in English. The first three attributions were proposed as options in the questionnaire; the others were inserted by the respondents. The figures do not refer to percentages but to numbers of individual learners.

Table 4.1
Attributions indicated by 30 learners dissatisfied with their progress in English

	"Unsuccessful" students	"Successful" students
1. Insufficient effort or other temporary shortcomings	8	5
2. Distraction of personal problems or practical difficulties (timetable, travelling etc.)	4	6
3. No aptitude for studying languages or the English language in particular	4	2
4. Cannot find the right study method	1	0
5. Inadequacies of the teachers	1	4
6. Too many students in the class	0	1
7. Textbook too easy	0	1
8. Poor organization within the institution	0	3
9. Level of course not high enough	0	1
10. Little opportunity to speak during lessons	0	2

Considering these attributions in the light of Weiner's model cited above, no. 1 suggests an internal cause that is unstable and controllable, and therefore reversible should the learner elect to display greater commitment in the future. No. 2 is external and uncontrollable, while no. 3 is internal, stable and uncontrollable. Of the attributions suggested by the respondents themselves, nos. 4-10, only no. 4 is an internal cause, and even then the learner could complain that at least part of the responsibility lies with the teachers who have not helped her identify the best way to study.

Only six learners dissatisfied with their past performance cited their own inability as the primary problem (no. 3), thirteen admitted to personal but temporary shortcomings (no. 1) while 23 pointed to external causes (no. 2 + nos. 5-10). These findings are therefore entirely in line with those of Ushioda (2003) and Williams *et al* (2001) cited above, and they confirm the importance of acceptable spin or benign self-delusion as a strategy to enable learners to maintain their motivation in the face of failure, even repeated failure.

It is worth noting that respondents who were dissatisfied but nevertheless relatively successful (according to the institution's criteria but not necessarily their own) volunteered far more attributions than their classmates who had not yet passed the first year exam. There is evidence that some felt that they were not being pushed hard enough: one considered the textbook too easy and another rated the level of the course too low. Attributions of this nature help us interpret the finding that the Lmed students, though still the most successful in terms of examination results, were the ones who reported loss of desire to learn English. According to expectancy-value theories, motivation to perform a task is the product not just of expectancy of success, but also of the importance someone attaches to achieving success in that task. It could be argued, therefore, that if the task is seen as too easy, it is devalued in the learner's mind, and as a consequence motivation is weakened. Similarly, Locke and Latham's (1990) goal-setting theory states that the more difficult the goal, the greater the learner's sense of achievement. So it is possible that learners who began with the expectation that they would have to work hard but in return would accomplish worthy achievements actually became demotivated because the institution's target does not represent a sufficient challenge.

That the dissatisfied and "unsuccessful" learners offered only two attributions of their own suggests that one reason for their lack of success might be insufficient appraisal of the learning situation and inadequate self-assessment during the actional phase of the learning process, a propensity for cognitive passivity which would lead to the non-application of action control measures and the failure to adopt strategies to get back on course for goal attainment. For the eight who accepted responsibility for their lack of success (attribution no. 1), it is difficult to see how the negative trend can be reversed without some measure of self-regulation, which must be preceded by appraisal. However, they have at least left the door open to future achievement, while the four who indicated that they had no aptitude for L2 learning might well be destined to fulfil their own pessimistic prophecy.

Table 4.2 reports on those learners who expressed some degree of satisfaction with their progress and how they accounted for their relative success.

Table 4.2

Attributions indicated by 70 learners satisfied with their progress in English

	Unsuccessful students	Successful students
1. Ability and/or other personal qualities (intelligence, powers of concentration etc.)	3	16
2. Capacity to study and learn despite certain practical difficulties	4	17
3. Self-motivation and/or ability to realise personal goals	6	14
4. Love of UK and/or English culture and society	1	1
5. Reading literature or watching films in English	0	1
6. Frequent trips to the UK	0	1
7. Use of the internet	0	1

Here too attributions 1-3 were given in the questionnaire while nos. 4-7 were volunteered by the respondents. With retrospect, it is evident that among the given attributions there should have been one that referred to the influence of a stimulating teacher or of a particularly well-organised course, i.e. of a clearly external cause. Of course, the respondents had the opportunity to cite such a cause in their own attributions, but none did so. In fact, the great majority attributed their relative success to the three internal attributions offered in the questionnaire, and once again this is in line with previous findings. Of the four attributions given by the respondents, nos. 4-6 indicate interest in and willingness to approach the target language culture and its speakers, i.e. integrative motivation.

Overall, phase 3 of the Cagliari survey revealed strong retention of desire to learn English even in the face of failure, or repeated failure, to achieve satisfactory outcomes in terms of examination results. Many of the learners investigated were still "wannabe L2 speakers", and their selection of internal, controllable attributions to account for poor past performance suggested that they believed they still had the potential to modify their behaviour sufficiently to achieve their goal. Potential is of little use without action, however, and just as lack of literal foraging will lead to hunger, so lack of metaphorical foraging will lead to learning failure. There may be some distance between how we really are (as learners or in any other role) and how we would like to be. Indeed, Higgins (1989) devised his *self-discrepancy theory* to explain the tensions beween our *actual self* (the person we really are), *our ideal self* (the person we would like to be) and our *ought self* (our understanding of what others want us to be). Extending this theory to second language acquisition, Csizer and Dörnyei (2005) suggest that inside each of us there is an *ideal language self*, and that L2 motivation is basically concerned with our endeavours to reduce the discrepancy between our actual language learning/speaking self and our ideal language self. The process of closing that gap entails internalising extrinsic motives (e.g. school-imposed targets become self-imposed targets) and cultivating an integrative disposition. Given the data produced in phases 1 to 3 of the survey, a focus on the learners' self-image seems appropriate for phase 4.

This project is concerned with accumulating data on the phenomenon of learners' motivation loss or retention over an extended period of time in the context of varying degrees of success. It does not seek to address matters of language teaching methodology or learning styles and strategies. For the institution concerned, however, the findings of the first three phases of the project would suggest that more needs to be done to provide on-going guidance for the young people who enrol on language degree courses, not just on what to study, but on how to study. The fact that in Table 4.2 above so few respondents cite out-of-classroom strategies to improve their L2 skills suggests that they have not acquired sufficient learner autonomy, something that ought to be a priority in a context in which the staff-to-student ratio requires learners to rely on their own resources to a considerable extent.

The next chapter will include a report of the fourth and final questionnaire administered in June 2011 when the successful learners, i.e. those who had remained on schedule to graduate after three years, were due to sit their final exams in English.

4.3 The Cagliari Case Study – phase 2

M and F were interviewed again on 11 May 2010, some nine months after the first meeting. The main purpose of the second interview was to discover how the two students rated their own performance over the preceding nine months and to question them about causal attributions. It should be recalled that their first year of studying English in the Faculty had culminated in very different outcomes: F had failed her end-of-year written test while M had passed the first year exam with the maximum score. Between the first and second interviews, F had failed the September re-sit before passing the written test at the third time of asking (January or February 2010) and then passing the subsequent oral exam at the first attempt. When the second interview took place, she was planning to take the second year exam the following month, and if she passed it she would be back on course to complete her studies within the official three-year duration of the course. M, in contrast, had taken a course outside the Faculty aimed at preparing learners for the Cambridge FCE (First Certificate in English) exam, an internationally recognised test at level B2 of the Common European Framework. She was due to take the FCE test the following month knowing that a pass would exempt her from having to take the second year written exam in the Faculty.

The first prompt asked them to comment on their degree of satisfaction with their progress in English over the preceding nine months. M was most satisfied and spoke approvingly of the second year general English lessons and of the teacher. From this answer it was clear that she had seen her FCE course as something in addition to rather than instead of the general English course in the Faculty, and summing the hours of the two courses meant that she had been getting quite a lot of contact time with native-speaker teachers. F described her satisfaction as '50-50'. She had had a different teacher for her second year English lessons and, unlike M, had not found the classroom activities particularly interesting or enjoyable.

The two students had no say in whose English classes they had to attend, and another external, uncontrollable factor that they cited (for the second time, since they had both mentioned it in phase 1) was the English department's failure to make use of the language labs. The simple institutional explanation for this is that the labs have a small number of work stations, the English classes are very big, and to try to subdivide those classes into "lab-sized" groups would create staffing and timetabling difficulties that outweigh the benefits of using the labs. From the students' perspective the issue is equally straightforward: an important resource, one which could be of great benefit to them, was not being used. In their appraisal of the learning situation, both F and M had identified an aspect of the educational context that they saw as an impediment to their goal attainment.

M and F were then asked esplicitly to name the factors that had had a positive effect on their learning of English and both mentioned virtually identical internal, controllable causal attributions. As Lcult students they had to read English literature as part of their course but both said they also read texts that were not on the syllabus. Both watched English-medium television, with F specifically mentioning *BBC World*. F also talked about the online version of *Speak Up*, a magazine for learners of English whose L1 is Italian. M's FCE course obviously brought her into contact with highly motivated learners and gave her the opportunity to practise her speaking skills in a way that was not possible in her large class in the Faculty. All of the above actions can be subsumed under the heading of extracurricular activities, and by now it was clear that in their willingness to commit themselves to much more than the minimum expected by the institution, M and F were active foragers who were unlikely to go short of mental pabulum. Their self-regulation and their propensity for taking the initiative in adopting L2-opportunity strategies marked them out as individuals engaged in the active process of learning rather than the passive process of being taught. In their case the three essential elements of the actional phase of the process model – subtask generation and implementation, ongoing appraisal and action control – were clearly functioning efficiently.

F and M appeared to have a positive image of themselves as serious students but both were constrained by modesty: asked to award themselves a mark between 1 and 10, both indicted 7 or 8.

Pressed to be more specific as regards their positive and negative qualities as learners, their self-assessments were practically identical. Both cited their regular attendance at nearly all lessons, and M also added that during the lessons she usually managed to remain attentive and focussed (the implication being that it would be easy to start daydreaming in certain lessons!). In many higher educational contexts, regular attendance is taken for granted; indeed it is often obligatory. As previously mentioned, that is not the case at M and F's institution, so their choosing to go to as many lessons as possible actually put them in a minority of particularly committed students.

As a negative quality, both indicated the difficulties they sometimes had in organising their time. They were perhaps being excessively self-critical here since their decision to attend practically all lessons in all subjects put demands upon their organisational skills that did not bother their colleagues who were less assiduous participants in class. That they had set themselves a tough schedule was evident in their response to the question regarding what factors sometimes prevented them from performing as they would have wished. Both admitted that they sometimes succumbed to fatigue and just had to take break.

They were then asked if they were influenced by their environment and the educational context, or whether they could study even when circumstances were not ideal. Both viewed themselves as autonomous learners with the ability to motivate themselves, and M considered herself a battler who did not allow logistical problems or organisational factors to hold her back.

On the question of when they expected to graduate, F said that she expected to go one year over the official three-year duration of the course. As previously noted, in Italian universities there is a long tradition of allowing "full-time" students to behave like part-timers and take the slow lane toward graduation, and to go *fuoricorso* by just one year is considered quite a commendable performance. For M everything depended on whether she decided to spend some months abroad on an Erasmus student exchange. During the first interview she had said that she would probably not apply for an Erasmus grant but nine months later she was having second thoughts. She was weighing up her options: if she stayed in Cagliari she would definitely get her degree within the three-year period; if she went on an Erasmus exchange, it would be an enjoyable and extremely useful experience, but she would probably (though not certainly) have to delay her graduation party by a year. Unlike a disturbing percentage of their fellow students, both clearly attached great importance to earning their degrees within a reasonable time span.

Asked about their plans for the future, M said that she wanted to take a higher level degree but would probably opt for mainland Italy rather than stay in Sardinia. She revealed her ambition in mentioning Urbino, a town in the Marche region that has around 16,000 permanent inhabitants and 20,000 students enrolled at its prestigious university. F's short-term plans included a trip to Amsterdam, where she expected to be able to use her English, and in the mid-term she hoped to find an opportunity to study and/or work in Germany for a few months. In both the first and second interviews, she made references to her German and it was clear that she had decided to give equal attention to the two languages of her course. In contrast, M did not mention her French and appeared (though she did not say so explicitly) to give priority to her English.

Finally, when invited to add comments of their own choosing, both pointed to something they had considered a positive aspect of the first year programme that had not been continued in the second year: the *tutorato*, i.e. the supplementary lessons conducted by the most impressive recent graduates. In making their appraisal of the learning situation, F and M had obviously appreciated the opportunity to have regular, contextualised contact with someone little older than themselves who had recently emerged successfully from the same educational process they were currently experiencing, and it struck them as perverse to discontinue something that clearly worked. The interviewer resisted the temptation to launch into a diatribe on public spending cuts.

From phase 1 of this case study, it was clear that F and M shared many positive characteristics as language learners but the question arose as to whether F would remain sufficiently motivated following the disappointing outcome after her first year of study (including the failed re-sit in September 2010). The evidence from phase 2 is that F had retained her linguistic self-confidence and was continuing to display self-regulated behaviour, autonomy, the ability to make a realistic appraisal of the learning situation and a willingness to take action control measures – in the form of various extracurricular activities – in order to reverse the trend towards unsatisfactory outcomes. In other words, her behaviour was similar to M's despite the setbacks encountered.

In terms of achievement, M and F had very different experiences after their first year in the Faculty. After the second year, things evened up a little. Shortly after the second interview, F passed her second year examination; the same strategies adopted to regain the ground lost in her first year had taken her on a roll leading to success at the next level. M was rewarded for her commitment outside the Faculty by a pass in the FCE test, which not only exempted her from the second year written exam, but also represented a useful addition to her curriculum vitae.

5 The Self in L2 motivation

The term *self* crops up in many attempts to explain motivation: the self-efficacy and self-worth theories mentioned in chapter 2, self-determination theory, the concepts of self-regulation and linguistic self-confidence, the individual's appraisal of the learning situation in relation to her self-image and her coping ability of Schumann's neurobiological model, the self-concept beliefs that are essential to the postactional phase of the process model, and to account for past performance the identification of causal attributions within or outside the self. Finally, as noted in the previous chapter, Csizer and Dörnyei (2005) place the concept of the ideal language self at the very heart of a theory of motivation. The term has also been recurrent in interpretations of the data generated in the Cagliari survey and the Cagliari case study, most notably to explain F's continued commitment to her L2 goal despite some disappointing results.

In focusing on the discrepancies between the actual self and the ideal self, Higgins (1989) and Csizer and Dörnyei are concerned with how an individual views him/herself as a unique individual, someone who may have similarities with but never be quite the same as anyone else on the planet. This we might call the personal self, and it is a fundamental element in a great deal of L2 motivation research. However, we also have an identity as a member of specific community, a social/cultural self. This kind of self has not been investigated to the same extent in the context of language learning but, as we will see below, it has not been entirely neglected. The section that follows summarises the findings from two studies of learners' self-images, one focusing on the personal self and the other on the social/cultural self. Views of self are then explored further in the final phases of the Cagliari survey and case study.

5.1 The personal Self and the social/cultural Self

Prior to her 2003 study cited in chapter 4, Ema Ushioda (2001) carried out research into the motivation of undergraduates not dissimilar to those investigated in the Cagliari survey and case study. Her subjects were twenty students of French at Trinity College Dublin and her research method involved structured interviews conducted in two stages separated by a period of 15-16 months. Her focus was on the learners' identification of causal attributions to explain past performance and the ways in which they maintained 'motivational thinking' even when achievement levels were not entirely satisfactory. She found that her subjects maintained a positive view of themselves as L2 learners through a highly selective approach to appraising past experience in which they highlighted the positive aspects and downplayed the significance of negative outcomes: 'The process of filtering experience and maintaining a positive belief structure seems to hinge in particular on sustaining a positive self-concept of personal ability or potential and on affirming a sense of motivational autonomy in the face of negative affective experiences' (*Ibid.*: 120). This summing up of the strategies employed by Irish undergraduates to maintain a positive self-image would be equally applicable to F's response to setbacks in phase 2 of the Cagliari case study.

Ushioda's analysis of the data from the two stages of interviews led to the identification of four patterns of causal attribution that contributed to the learners' maintenance of a positive view of themselves:

- enhancing one's self-concept by attributing positive L2 outcomes and achievement to a belief in personal ability or personal qualities (e.g., hard work, effort, a perfectionist approach);
- maintaining motivation through a belief in personal potential by attributing negative L2 outcomes or lack of success to temporary shortcomings that may be changed (e.g., lack of effort, lack of opportunity to spend time in an L2 environment);
- dissociating demotivating experiences from one's own underlying motivation for wanting to learn the L2 by attributing such negative affective experiences to the demerits of the institutionalized learning context (e.g., teaching methods, coursework pressures);

- believing in a capacity for self-motivation through personal resourcefulness and initiative in the face of the demotivating experiences of institutionalized learning (e.g., setting oneself goals, engaging in intrinsically motivating target language activity).

(Ushioda, 2001: 120)

Maintaining a positive self-concept will not in itself lead to positive outcomes unless it is accompanied by the appropriate commitment and effort. In any field and however great one's potential, if dreams are not translated into positive action one remains a "wannabe" until, with the passage of time, one becomes a "mightofbin". If, on the other hand, a sense of self-worth is translated into genuine motivational thinking and self-regulated behaviour, negative outcomes can be reversed and positive outcomes achieved (and in the context of L2 learning, F is the living proof). Conversely, if underlying self-belief is seriously weakened – if someone ends up thinking that she will never learn the target language because she just hasn't got what it takes – it is difficult to see how she will find the self-motivation required to invest the effort that is necessary to prevent an expectation of failure becoming a self-fulfilling prophecy.

However much we try to motivate language learners with creative teaching methods, interesting materials and lively classroom activities, ultimately it is the learners who must motivate themselves. Those with strong self-motivation can achieve success without lessons and without direct contact with speakers of the target language (I write with the experience of having met fluent English speakers who managed to learn the language in the Soviet Union).

Syed (2001) looked at self in terms of cultural identity in his case study of five learners (four US citizens and one Canadian) who had decided to study Hindi. Two were learning it as a foreign language and both had strong integrative motivation. The other three were learning Hindi as a *heritage language;* English was their first language but all three were ethnically Indian and for them learning Hindi represented a kind of journey of discovery of their cultural roots. Of these heritage learners, Suzy was born in Canada to immigrant parents from the former Portuguese colony of Goa in south-west India, Huma's family had left India when she was a small child and once in the United States she had lost her active skills in Hindi, and Rani was a second-generation immigrant who had never learnt Hindi although she had heard it spoken by relatives.

For Suzy, Huma and Rani, 'Learning Hindi […] allows these heritage learners a pathway into their heritage culture' (Syed, 2001: 137). In explaining their reasons for wishing to learn this language (*Ibid.*: 136, 137), all three express sentiments to the effect that not speaking Hindi gives them the sensation that something is missing from their cultural identity, and they note that their encounters with others repeatedly remind them of this missing element. They all have the physical characteristics of Indians, and as a consequence people expect them to know Hindi and are surprised and/or disappointed when it emerges that they do not. Huma and Rani use the adjectives "embarrassed" and "ashamed", and the latter describes a visit to India in which relatives she had never seen before did not hide their dismay at discovering that she could not communicate in the language of the extended family. Suzy, whose parents had facilitated her integration into Canadian society by speaking English at home, notes that she is always having to explain herself to people who "see my brown skin and assume I can speak the language".

All three also see knowledge of the Hindi language as a prerequisite for trying to understand the history, culture(s), family structures, religions and conflicts of the India their parents left:

> Heritage membership, something that has been tugging at them for some time, is now being realized and exercised through language study. It is very emotional, immediate, and personal for them. Suzy, Huma, and Rani also talked emotionally about their visits to India. It was "shocking," "revealing," and an "eye opening" experience for them. For Huma and Rani, it was a way to explore and identify with their culture. As Huma explains, "I like the kind of values and things that my culture teaches. I like Hinduism in itself; I like what it teaches you. I'm proud of that... I wanted to learn more about it, to experience it... it makes me closer to my roots."
>
> (*Ibid.*: 141)

Huma's commitment to learning Hindi goes beyond completion of her own cultural self: "I want to make sure I learn it so when I have kids I can keep the language going" (*Ibid.*: 137).

The desire to learn a heritage language is a common phenomenon among second-generation immigrants and first-generation immigrants who left their native land in early childhood, but usually only when they have grown up. Children are conformists and generally do not want to be noticeably different from their schoolmates, which explains both the rapid acquisition of the language of the host country and the loss of the parents' first language. In adulthood, people are less concerned about not being conspicuous, indeed may wish to emphasise their otherness. The commitment to acquiring that heritage language involves deep emotions and questions of identity that do not form part of the motivational matrix of the learner of a foreign language.

5.2 The Cagliari Survey – phase 4

The fourth and final stage of the survey was conducted in June 2011 and, as usual, in order to have feedback from as many respondents as possible, the questionnaire was administered when the students were about to sit their written examinations in English in one or other of the two sessions in that month. All students who had enrolled in

2008-09 were asked to complete the questionnaire irrespective of whether they were due to take the 3rd year exam or re-sit either the 2nd or the 1st year test, so it was possible to distinguish between those who were up-to-date in their English studies, those who had fallen behind schedule and those who had made no measurable progress in English since the start of their course. The subjects investigated fell into three groups:

- GROUP A (25 people): students who could be considered successful because they were about to take the 3rd year exam and were therefore on schedule.
- GROUP B (19 people): students whose achievement was unsatisfactory because they had not yet passed the 2nd year exam despite having had up to three opportunities to sit it during the preceding year.
- GROUP C (21 people): spectacularly unsuccessful students who were going to sit the 1st year exam, possibly for the seventh time.

In many countries the idea of allowing a university student who has failed the same examination six times to re-enrol is absolutely unthinkable. In Italy, just as no one bats an eyelid if someone requires eight years to complete a three-year degree course, so nobody gets excessively fussed if a student comes back to try a specific exam for the tenth time. For twenty years I have been questioning Italian colleagues about the wisdom of persevering with this policy, but by way of reply I have seldom received more than a resigned shrug of the shoulders. The consequence in this case is that of 65 undergraduates who enrolled in 2008-09, 40 were behind schedule as regards their English language exams, and of those 40, 21 had made no progress at all.

When the first questionnaire was administered during lessons in October 2008, 150 students completed it. By June 2011 only 65 of the 2008-09 intake were present for important examinations, which meant that nearly 57% of the original population had either dropped out or, if still officially enrolled, were no longer active students. The 25 who were still on schedule with their English exams represented just 17% of the class of 2008-09. The very least one can say about such a system is that it is wasteful.

The variables of age and sex were not statistically significant in relation to achievement. Both starting level of English and choice of degree course, however, were found to be closely correlated to exam success. Although Groups A, B and C consisted of 25, 19 and 21 students respectively, a few did not complete the biodata on the questionnaire, and as a consequence the numbers for group totals in the following table are 23, 18 and 20.

Table 5.1: The Cagliari survey phase 4 – the impact of starting level and choice of degree on achievement

	Group A	Group B	Group C
Starting level: Elementary	4/23	1/18	10/20
Starting level: Pre-intermediate	16/23	13/18	8/20
Starting level: Intermediate +	3/23	4/18	2/20
Choice of degree: Lcom	1/23	7/18	12/20
Choice of degree: Lcult	14/23	6/18	3/20
Choice of degree: Lmed	8/23	5/18	5/20

The definition of starting level depended on the respondents' own assessments rather than objective measurement, and this accounts for the illogical claim by two of the Group C students that their starting level was at least intermediate even though they had repeatedly failed an examination at pre-intermediate level. Most made realistic assessments, however, and it emerges that in half the cases of zero progress the learners concerned had been inadequately prepared at the beginning of the course and had not managed to get up to standard (a remedial course for complete beginners had been provided but not everyone who needed it attended the lessons). That four of the Group A students had also started with little or no English demonstrates that autonomous, self-regulated learners could overcome this initial handicap.

The figures for choice of degree course are startling. In phase 1 the Lmed students had appeared the most motivated and those most likely to succeed but in subsequent phases their "superiority" was shown to be on the wane. By phase 4 they had been decisively overtaken by those enrolled on the Lcult course. For those on the Lcom course the situation is dramatic with more than half of the respondents having made no measurable progress in English since enrolling 33 months earlier. Speculating as to why the Lcom students had achieved so little in developing their L2 skills, it is possible that from the beginning they had been more attracted to the media studies element of the degree course than to the study of two languages. Similarly, the higher achievement of the Lcult students (in relative terms; there were still nine re-sitting exams) might be attibutable to the overall nature of the degree course; lecturers throughout the world complain that young people who grew up with the internet are skilled at scanning short texts for specific information but are not trained in sustained analytical reading, but the traditional nature of the Lcult course, with its emphasis on literature, obliges undergraduates to read and interpret longer texts in old-fashioned books, an exercise that has the happy spin-off of developing their lexicogrammatical competence.

Question 1 asked the respondents to report directly on their self-image. The three optional responses were designed to distinguish between students with a very positive self-image, those entertaining doubts as to whether they would achieve their goal, and people whose appraisal of their own performance had persuaded them to adopt a less ambitious goal.

Table 5.2: The Cagliari survey phase 4 – Q1: Indicate the sentence that best represents how you see yourself.

	Group A	*Group B*	*Group C*
A. I would like to become really good at English and I think I'm on the way to achieving that objective	16/25	5/19	10/21
B. I would like to become really good at English but I don't think I'm making the progress necessary to make my wish come true	8/25	12/19	9/21
C. I don't expect to become really good at English. I know my limits	1/25	2/19	2/21

It is astonishing that in such a desolate situation as regards achievement, only five of the 65 respondents had resigned themselves to having to aim for a downgraded goal, and it says a great deal about our capacity to attribute poor past performance either to external causes or to internal causes that we can influence if we make up our minds to do so. Indeed, ten of the 21 "serial failures" in Group C had retained a very positive self-image, which is indicative of an enormous gap between their ideal language self and their actual self. Most of the Group B respondents had doubts about their ability to achieve their L2 goal but only two indicated resignation. Unsurprisingly, most of the successful students of Group A had a postive self-image, although one indicated she would never be a particularly good user of English. After checking this response against her biodata, it emerged that she had also begun the course with only elementary knowledge of English, which meant that her success in staying on schedule was particularly commendable. As noted earlier, however, the learner's criteria for achievement do not always coincide with those of the educational institution.

Question 2 was designed to understand the respondents' learning behaviour, with options to distinguish between students with little appetite for the necessary but sometimes tedious aspects of language study, those who stuck at the task out of a sense of duty and people who claimed to derive genuine enjoyment from the learning process even when it was hard work.

Table 5.3: The Cagliari survey phase 4 – Q2: Indicate the sentence that best represents your point of view.

	Group A	*Group B*	*Group C*
A. I think studying a foreign language should be enjoyable. If I get bored I stop studying	4/25	7/19	5/20*
B. Because of my parents I feel I have a duty to study English properly even when I don't really feel like it	2/25	1/19	2/20*
C. I study English willingly. Sometimes it's hard work but it's rewarding all the same	19/25	11/19	13/20*

* One respondent invaliadated her response on this item by indicating two options

The majority of Group B and Group C respondents clearly imagined their ideal language selves as highly motivated individuals who found the learning process a pleasurable experience, although it beggars belief to accept that thirteen people who had truly studied English willingly, and had found the endeavour rewarding, should have zero achievement after 33 months. The poor results suggest that a more sincere self-assessment of learning behaviour would have seen many more respondents indicating option A, but admitting to such a dilettante approach obviously conflicted with their self-image. All but five of the respondents should hope that their parents never see Table 5.3.

Question 3 invited the respondents to indicate a degree of (dis)satisfaction with past experiences of studying English at school or university. This item gave unsuccessful learners the opportunity to attribute their poor achievement to the demerits of the educational istitutions they had attended.

Table 5.4: The Cagliari survey phase 4 – Q3: Up to now your experiences of studying English at school and/or university have been:

	Group A	Group B	Group C
A. definitely positive	5/25	2/19	3/21
B. more positive than negative	18/25	9/19	8/21
C. more negative than positive	2/25	8/19	10/21
D. definitely negative	0/25	0/19	0/21

Although more respondents in Groups B and C reported negative experiences compared with Group A, it is perhaps surprising that a greater number did not attribute their lack of achievement to an external, uncontrollable cause. The correlation between success and positive perceptions of past learning experiences is clear from the data for Group A, but it is also apparent that many of the low achievers did not seek to load all the blame for their poor performance on teachers and institutions. These figures confirm those in Table 4.1 in the previous chapter, which showed that unsuccessful learners were more likely to attribute their results to lack of effort or other temporary shortcomings than to the educational context.

If question 1 sought to find out how the respondents saw themselves generally in terms of ability and potential, question 4 focused on more specific L2 learning skills, such as the ability to organise one's time and the use of appropriate strategies.

Table 5.5: The Cagliari survey phase 4 – Q4: Which sentence describes you best?

	Group A	Group B	Group C
A. I know how to study English. I use various learning strategies and I am able to organise my time	9/25	4/19	5/21
B. I think I'm capable of reaching a good level of English but I need advice on how to study effectively	15/25	15/19	15/21
C. It isn't a question of methods or strategies. I'm just not really cut out for learning English	1/25	0/19	1/21

Out of a total of 65 respondents, 45 reported that they needed advice on how to study in such a way as to realise their potential. To an extent L2 learners have always dreamt of discovering a "magic method" that would make their arduous, long-term task painless and fast, and purveyors of self-study courses know that a certain number of consumers will always give credence to the promise that they can "learn French in a month with our revolutionary new system". However, it is also reasonable to assume that many of the subjects of this survey did indeed require guidance on how to make the transition from the highly structured, teacher-led context of school to a university system in which they were suddenly expected to be self-regulated and to assume responsibility for the organisation of their learning. That only two people indicated that they had no real aptitude for L2 learning demonstrates that practically all the respondents maintained an image of themselves as able and potentially successful learners, but most attributed their actual performance to not having found (or not having been taught) the surefire method to transform all that potential into concrete achievement.

Five of the Group C students believed that they had no need to be advised on how to study since they already knew what learning strategies to adopt and how to organise their time. A cross-check revealed that the same five individuals had indicated in question 1 that they believed they were on their way to becoming really good at English, further testament to the power of selective, highly subjective assessment of performance to permit people to maintain a positive self-image even when all the objective evidence suggests that their actual achievements are negligible. At times the discrepancy between the ideal language self and the actual self is not so much a gap as a chasm.

Another cross-check showed that the Group A respondent who believed that she was just not cut out for language learning was the same student who had indicated in question 1 that she did not expect ever to become a good user of English. As noted above, since her English was at elementary level when she enrolled, her achievement in staying on schedule with her exams was praiseworthy. Furthermore, she was one of the very few respondents to indicate that she stuck at her studies out of a sense of duty to her parents rather than because she derived pleasure from the learning process. While several students had maintained an astonishingly positive self-image given their appalling results, this young lady had a low opinion of herself as a learner despite having made commendable progress. The advantage of anonymity in a survey is that respondents have no reason to fear repercussions if they state exactly what they think; the disadvantage is that if it is revealed that an individual needs help – and the learner in question would certainly benefit from a few warm words to boost her self-esteem – it is impossible to intervene.

5.3 The Cagliari Survey – conclusions

The high drop-out rate in Italian universities has been mentioned repeatedly in these reports of the Cagliari survey and it is worth summing up the factors that account for Italy's getting such a poor return on its investment in higher education:

- because there is no obligatory link between subject specialisation at high school and choice of degree course, many new undergraduates sign up to courses for which they lack the appropriate background and then suffer the disheartening experience of discovering that they are ill-prepared for the demands of the degree they have chosen;
- low tuition fees lower students' sense of duty to their parents and encourage the practice of "giving university a try" without the need to make a real psychological commitment;
- in Italy many young people go to their local university and often continue to live with their parents, so enrolling at university does not have the life-changing "rite of passage" associations of a similar decision in a country such as the UK;
- there is no stigma attached to falling behind schedule, even by several years, and the absence of maintenance grants or student loans means that there are no serious financial penalties involved.

The purpose of the Cagliari survey was not to investigate the national phenomenon of high drop-out rates, however, but to study developments over time in the motivation of a specific group of learners. Again, the main findings can be summarised:

- most of the subjects started with high desire to learn English and this goal was maintained over time;
- that having a goal is not the same as having motivation is evinced in learning outcomes that suggest that for many subjects the goal was not supported by the necessary effort (i.e. in terms of Dörnyei and Ottó's process model, intention formation in the preactional phase was not translated into intention enactment in the actional phase);
- nearly all the subjects, including those with low achievement, maintained a positive self-image and underlying self-belief, primarily by attributing poor past performance to temporary shortcomings that were in their power to put right;
- only a minority attributed poor performance to external causes such as the educational environment or the inadequacy of the teachers;
- for reasons that could not be ascertained in quantitative research of this nature, students enrolled on the *Lingue e comunicazione* degree course had poorer learning outcomes (in English language at any rate) than those who had opted for one of the other courses offered by the institution.

The overall picture is grim: 150 students completed the phase 1 questionnaire in October 2008, but 33 months later only 65 were present for phase 4 even though the fourth questionnaire was administered on examination days when the subjects had a powerful incentive to go into the Faculty. Of those 65, only 25 were on schedule with their English examinations. It is essentially a story not of language learning, but of failure to learn, with students who exhibit an enormous discrepancy between their ideal language selves and their actual selves. The L2 goal remains intact but, from the evidence of the results obtained, not accompanied by genuine motivation in the form of commitment, perseverance, self-regulation or autonomous learning behaviour.

This survey has also demonstrated one of the recurrent pitfalls of research based on self-report data, i.e. that the respondents' subjective perceptions of themselves may be at odds with their actual behaviour. Phase 1 appeared to show most of the subjects having very high intrinsic motivation, but subsequent achievement data from examination scores revealed that although they had a strong desire to learn English, many were not committed to effecting the intention enactment required to pass on to the actional phase of the learning process. In short, they were attracted to the idea of learning the target language but were less keen on dressing their dream in work clothes. Ideally, self-report data should be verified by studies of actual behaviour, but since some, if not most, L2 learning occurs outside the classroom, it would be neither practicable nor ethical to monitor people's learning behaviour in extracurricular contexts.

5.4 The Cagliari Case Study – phase 3

The third interviews took place in June (with M) and July (with F) 2011. By this time F had passed her third year written exam in English, which meant that she had made up all the lost ground after her difficult first year and was back on schedule with her English exams (although this was not the case for German). M had spent some months in Dublin on an Erasmus student exchange and while in Ireland she had taken an examination that substituted the third year English test in Cagliari.

Both expressed satisfaction with the progress they had made since enrolling at the Faculty, although M was at pains to add that she wanted to improve her English still further. Once again they attributed their past performance to extracurricular activities, with F citing her studies in the Language Centre and her preference for watching Hollywood films in the original version, while M mentioned her reading of novels, magazines and newspapers. M had found her stay in Dublin extremely useful and said that she sought opportunities to speak English with foreigners resident in Cagliari.

M and F felt that their motivation to learn English had increased since they had started the course and F added that it had been particularly satisfying to see her hard work rewarded by improved results.

As noted earlier in this work, the Cagliari survey and case study took place against a backdrop of economic crisis in the nation and considerable turbulence in Italian universities owing to public spending cuts and a controversial reform of higher education. Neither saw this context as an impediment. M said that her self-discipline and methodical approach had enabled her to ignore the problems and remain focused on achieving her goals. F felt that the difficult circumstances had actually acted as a stimulus in that the confusion all about her had made her even more determined to show what she could do. At this point it is worth noting that in phase 3 of the Cagliari survey, when respondents were invited to state the causes to which they attributed their past performance, not one cited the general economic and political context or specific consequences in the Faculty (e.g. understaffing). M felt that there had not been any significant obstacles to her making progress, although she acknowledged that she was fortunate to live near the university and not have to contend with public transport. F mentioned health problems but also said she had not been hindered by logistical or organisational difficulties.

Asked to indicate their strong and weak points as students, F said that her positive qualities included independence and her critical and self-critical approach (i.e. ongoing appraisal), and on the negative side felt that she had missed opportunities to meet and speak English with foreign students on Erasmus exchanges in Cagliari. M considered herself serious, autonomous and committed. She said she sometimes tried to take on too much – for instance, she might plan to sit too many exams in a specific session – and then had to revise her plans when the strain got to her. M considered this a demerit. An objective observer might argue that setting oneself challenging short- and midterm goals is actually an excellent self-motivation strategy.

When questioned about their plans for the future, F said she wanted to work as an au pair in Germany. As mentioned above, she was not on schedule with her German exams, and having taken decisive action to reverse a trend of negative outcomes in English, she was obviously determined to deal with her other language in a similarly effective manner. Both said they would like to take a higher degree, either on the Italian mainland or abroad. M's ambition was to teach Italian abroad. She returned to the subject of her stay in Dublin, which had not just helped her improve her communicative skills, but had also given her a taste for experiencing a different cultural environment.

5.5 The Cagliari Case Study – conclusions

The Cagliari Survey ended up as a study of L2 learners who thought they were motivated but actually were not since their goals and intentions were not converted into appropriate actions, and in the majority of cases that lack of real motivation was reflected in poor learning outcomes. In contrast, the two subjects of the Cagliari Case Study proved to be exceptionally well-motivated, and their commitment led to positive achievement, albeit after initial setbacks and the taking of action control measures in F's case. In retrospect, it can be said that M and F were always likely to exhibit high motivation because of the circumstances in which the case study began; they were not chosen at random but responded to my appeal for volunteers, and the mere act of agreeing to help me immediately marked them out as two people interested in understanding themselves as language learners and willing to do more than the minimum required by the educational institution. It could not have been otherwise; given the extraordinarily high drop-out rate, had I chosen subjects at random, I might have ended up with two people who disappeared off the radar after the first interview. In contrast, the two volunteers literally stayed the course, cooperated willingly and have both expressed a strong desire to read the report of the investigation.

M and F are good language learners because they are active learners. In their ongoing appraisal of the learning situation, they identify ways in which they can complement their study in the Faculty with extracurricular activities that increase their exposure to the target language (spoken and/or written) and enable them to hone their communicative skills. Both have a positive self-image, but unlike many who enrolled at the same time, they are actively engaged in investing the time and effort required to close the gap between their actual selves and their ideal language selves. F responded well to the disappointment of negative initial outcomes by attributing her lack of success not to external causes over which she had no control, but by assuming responsibility and changing her learning behaviour to turn things around. M suffered no such setbacks, which may or may not mean that she has greater aptitude for language learning; she obviously works quite as hard as F does, so her positive achievements are essentially the product of a genuine commitment to realising her goals.

Both F and M are autonomous, self-regulated learners who adopt a variety of learning and motivational strategies while the majority of their fellow students, including some who are relatively successful, report that they lack an effective learning method. Unlike a school, a university rightly expects its undergraduates to be autonomous learners who do not require constant monitoring. However, a case could be made for setting up introductory "learning how to learn" sessions for new students at the start of their first year. M and F both spoke positively of the *tutorato* system of supplementary lessons conducted by recent graduates, and one can see how newly enrolled youngsters could benefit from insights given from a student's perspective by people who had achieved success. Instead of academic staff, the ideal people to lead such "learning how to learn" sessions might be students like F and M, particularly the former with her experience of taking action to reverse negative trends. Of course, students can be told about learning strategies but cannot be obliged to use them. Whether motivation itself can be taught is also open to question, and it is a matter that is addressed in the next chapter.

6 The influence of age, gender and learning environment on motivation

Where language learning is concerned, stereotypes abound, as does anecdotal evidence that appears to disprove them. It makes intuitive sense to assume that children are more motivated learners than adults because they are naturally curious about the world around them, until a teacher tells you about pupils whose lethargy borders on ataraxy, or you meet a senior citizen who, to keep his/her brain active after retirement, learnt an additional language. Everybody has been to school, so everyone feels entitled to make generalisations about the attitudes and learning potential of male or female pupils, generalisations that are not always supported by solid empirical data. Similarly, practically everyone has views about what schools and teachers should do to stimulate and maintain learners' motivation, although after a little questioning it often emerges that what they suggest would have been perfect for them as individuals, but not necessarily for other students. In this chapter, we will try to avoid stereotypes and look at what research tells us.

6.1 Age, second language acquisition and motivation

We noted in chapter 2 that a distinction is sometimes made between acquisition, the unconscious process of picking up a language through interaction with speakers of it, and language learning, the conscious process of studying and trying to absorb the lexical, grammatical and pragmatic norms of the target language. Obviously, children do not learn their native language; they acquire it, and nearly always do so quickly and efficiently (an exception was little Albert Einstein, whose parents feared he might be retarded because he suffered from language delay). Because we pick up our first language so effortlessly – indeed, children brought up in a bilingual family acquire two with no apparent difficulty – but struggle with a second language and rarely reach the level of a native speaker, it has been speculated that after a certain age, the painless process of acquisition gives way to learning. In formulating his *Critical Period Hypothesis* (CPH), Lenneberg (1967: 176) suggested that, 'Automatic acquisition from mere exposure to a given language seems to disappear [after puberty], and foreign languages have to be taught and learned though a conscious and labored effort'. Similarly, proponents of the theory of *Universal Grammar* (UG) – 'the system of principles, conditions, and rules that are elements or properties of all human languages' (Chomsky, 1976: 29) – claim that first languages are acquired easily because children's innate knowledge of the universal principles of language merely has to be triggered, while other cognitive processes are involved in the case of second languages. Over the years both Universal Grammar and the Critical Period Hypothesis have been elaborated upon, revised and openly challenged, but the majority of researchers believe that there are maturational constraints at work in learning/acquiring languages. It also makes sense in evolutionary terms to suppose that a faculty for rapid language acquisition would be deactivated once it were no longer needed.

Just because a goal is difficult to achieve, it does not necessarily follow that we are not motivated to strive towards it. On the contrary, if man did not relish a challenge he would never have crossed oceans or scaled mountains, and as we have already seen in Locke and Latham's goal-setting theory, the more difficult the goal, the greater our sense of achievement. When the goal is language learning, the age factor in relation to motivation has been investigated, and by now it will come as no surprise to learn that a particularly relevant research project was carried out in Canada.

MacIntyre *et al* (2003) studied English-speaking pupils in grades 7, 8 and 9 (ages 12-14) of a high school in Nova Scotia who had volunteered to join French immersion classes. The aim of the study was to investigate the influence of sex and age on the pupils' willingness to communicate (WTC), anxiety, perceived competence in French, and L2 motivation. The sample consisted of 96 boys and 188 girls. The age range 12-14 is interesting since students entering or about to enter puberty are particularly susceptible to swings in learning behaviour as in other types of behaviour. For some, though not all, CPH researchers, puberty is also thought to mark the end of the critical period.

To sum up their findings as regards the effect of age:

- anxiety levels remained fairly constant over the three grades;
- WTC, perceived competence and frequency of communication in French increased between grades 7 and 8, then remained steady between grades 8 and 9;
- L2 motivation (as measured by the Attitude/Motivation Index [AMI], an adapted form of Gardner's AMTB) dropped between grades 7 and 8 and did not rise again in grade 9.

The paradox of higher perceptions of L2 competence plus greater use of French and improved willingness to speak it despite falling motivation is difficult to interpret. In volunteering to join an immersion class, these pupils had demonstrated high initial motivation, and their good performance between grades 7 and 8 might have been expected to reinforce that motivation. One explanation is that the AMI data reflect something other than specifically L2 motivation. As the authors themselves acknowledge: 'It is […] possible that the decrease in motivation […] reflects a more global decrease in achievement motivation among adolescent learners and not one specific to language learning' (*Ibid.*: 160). As parents and teachers know only too well, the surge in self-consciousness that accompanies puberty often leads young people to the conviction that exhibiting too much enthusiasm for school work puts them at risk of losing face with their peers.

These findings also raise a question regarding the relationship between achievement and motivation. While motivation impacts positively on achievement, the reverse is not necessarily true if someone does not value highly whatever has been achieved. Since the subjects of this study were in a full immersion situation, they could hardly fail to improve their French, but if for these adolescents other goals had become more urgent than that of L2 acquisition, it is not entirely surprising if their motivation had declined.

6.2 Gender and L2 motivation

Approximately 80% of the students investigated in the Cagliari survey were female and two thirds of the pupils in MacIntyre *et al*'s study (above) were girls. Gardner (1985b) reports that in L2 educational contexts girls tend to outperform boys and argues that their superior achievement is the consequence of more positive attitudes towards language learning. In universities in the United States and much of Europe the recent trend has been for female students to enrol on degree courses traditionally seen as disciplines dominated by men, such as physics or engineering, but there has been no corresponding increase in male undergraduates studying modern languages, a field by convention dominated by women. It is interesting to note, however, that in our section on exceptional language learners in chapter 1, all the hyperpolyglots mentioned are men. It is possible, therefore, that female L2 superiority applies to learning but not to acquisition.

Research findings in the field are anything but uniform. Ellis (2008: 313-314) cites a number of investigations that showed female learners exhibiting higher motivation and/or more positive attitudes: in a major study of 6,000 English children, Burstall (1975) found that the girls consistently demonstrated more favourable attitudes towards learning L2 French than the boys did; Gardner and Lambert (1972) found that female learners of L2 French in Canada had both higher L2 motivation and more positive attitudes toward the target language community; Spolsky (1989) reported that female learners of L2 Hebrew in Israel displayed more favourable attitudes toward the target language; Bacon and Finnemann (1992) found that female university students of L2 Spanish had higher instrumental motivation. MacIntyre *et al* (2003: 143) cite Worrall and Tsarna (1987) who found that girls' superior achievement and attitudes could be linked to the behaviour of their teachers, who, irrespective of whether they were men or women themselves, tended to have higher expectations of girls and consequently gave them more encouragement and advice. A smaller but nevertheless significant number of studies have produced quite different results, however. For instance, in a study of learners of L2 French, German or Spanish at tertiary level, Ludwig (1983) found that male students had higher instrumental motivation.

All the studies referred to above investigated L2 learners in formal education at school or university, and as noted in the preceding section, there is always the risk that data gathered to gauge attitudes toward language learning actually reflect more general attitudes regarding education, institutions and teachers. Work on informal acquisition often focuses on adult immigrants, and here a number of studies suggest that men outperform women, but again (though for quite different reasons) we should be wary of accepting all findings at face value. Evidence of differences in L2 achievement, attitudes and motivation related to gender (which is socially defined) do not necessarily mean that there are similar differences related to sex (which is biologically defined). Ellis (2008: 314), for instance, notes that among first-generation Asian immigrants in Britain, males are usually more successful at acquiring English, but points out that this is simply the consequence of their traditional gender roles: the male breadwinners have opportunities to interact with English speakers while the female homemakers spend most of their time using L1 with their children or their fellow Asians who run the neighbourhood shops. When their children attend school, their daughters might well pick up English faster than their sons.

The investigation by MacIntyre *et al* reported in the previous section looked at the influence of sex as well as age. The subjects of the study were approaching or already experiencing 'the wonders of puberty' (MacIntyre *et al*, 2003: 138), and given that girls usually reach puberty before boys do, it is reasonable to assume that there was some interaction between the effects of sex and age. Indeed, the authors speculate that one of their findings – that the girls had lower anxiety, with a notable drop in anxiety between grades 8 and 9 – might be attributable to that interaction: 'Grade 9 girls might be past the most anxiety-provoking phase of puberty, perhaps making them less anxious and more willing to communicate' (*Ibid.*: 158). On the willingness-to-communicate scale, the girls had higher values throughout the three years of the study, a factor the authors suspect could be related to the aforementioned discovery by Worrall and Tsarna (1987) that there is a tendency for girls 'to find favor in the classroom' (*Ibid.*: 159). Their conclusion, however, is that the effects of differential treatment were not of an order that put the male students at a significant disadvantage.

Similar methods and similar subjects were involved in Baker and MacIntyre's (2003) investigation of the effects of gender on learners of L2 French on either immersion or non-immersion programmes on the predominantly English-speaking island of Cape Breton. A total of 195 students with ages ranging from 14 to 18 were monitored, 71 who had opted for an immersion programme and 124 studying French in non-immersion classes. The immersion programme obviously entailed prolonged exposure to the target language and contact with native speakers, while both exposure time and contact were limited in the case of normal classes, so the choice of programme had parallels with the study of French as a second language or as a foreign language. The factors explored were: perceived competence in French, willingness to communicate in French, frequency of communication, communication anxiety, reasons for studying French (from the four options of getting a job, travelling, meeting francophones and personal achievement), and attitude/motivation (again measured by the Attitude/Motivation Index).

One might expect learners opting for an immersion programme to have high integrative motivation, but the picture that emerged from Baker and MacIntyre's study was not as straightforward as that. Although there was the predictable immersion/non-immersion dichotomy for the communication variables, the AMI scores showed that the female non-immersion students had similar attitudes towards French as the immersion students. The male non-immersion students, in contrast, had significantly lower attitude levels (*Ibid.*: 88).

Unexpected findings also emerged on the question of reasons for studying French. The female non-immersion students actually scored higher than the immersion students on the options of travelling and meeting francophones (both indicative of an integrative orientation) and personal satisfaction (which suggests intrinsic motivation). In fact, on wishing to meet francophones the female immersion students had lower orientations than the male non-immersion students (*Ibid.*: 89), a result that challenges commonly cherished stereotypes about females being more socially oriented. The male immersion students showed the highest job-related orientation, which suggests high instrumental motivation and is possibly indicative of a traditional view of gender roles as regards the job market.

The authors point out that the 'limited research concerning gender differences in second language acquisition makes it difficult to surmise why these findings occurred or if they could be replicated in another sample' (*Ibid.*: 89). Given the persistent imbalance between the numbers of male and female learners signing up to language courses, it is to be hoped that that will be rectified in the near future.

6.3 The influence of the learning environment

At the beginning of this work we noted that there is no shortage of self-help books and websites that seek to convince us that we are all capable of extraordinary achievements if we just invest the modest sum required to be given access to the secrets to motivating ourselves, and that once properly motivated we will finally be able to tap the potential within us. Similarly, teachers want nothing more than to find the magic formula that will motivate underperforming students and knock down the psychological and behavioural barriers blocking their path to success. In reality, there are no secrets or magic formulae since motivation is a complex, multi-faceted phenomenon that does not lend itself to quick fixes. That said, it is undeniable that the various aspects of the learning environment – first and foremost the teacher, but also materials, tasks, class dynamics and the classroom ambience – all have an effect on the learner's enthusiasm and commitment, and education professionals have a duty to remove potential obstacles to learning whenever possible. Dörnyei and Csizér (1998: 215) have proposed 'Ten commandments for motivating language learners':

1. Set a personal example with your own behaviour.
2. Create a pleasant, relaxed atmosphere in the classroom.
3. Present the tasks properly.
4. Develop a good relationship with the learners.
5. Increase the learner's linguistic self-confidence.
6. Make the language classes interesting.
7. Promote learner autonomy.
8. Personalise the learning process.
9. Increase the learners' goal-orientedness.
10. Familiarise learners with the target language culture.

It is often advisable to be suspicious of neat lists of ten items, especially if they are labelled "ten commandments". Those of us who have never coveted our neighbour's ox or manservant do not give equal weight to all ten commandments listed in *Exodus* 20, and in Dörnyei and Csizér's list there are some items that are so self-evident to any teacher with a smidgen of professionalism that they scarcely need to be stated (numbers 1-4 and number 6). Perhaps we need to be reminded of number 5 and the need to make judicious use of praise, numbers 7-9 and the desirability of giving learners some choice (and, therefore, also responsibility) in the learning process, and number 10, which has the potential to boost integrative motivation. We might also add an 11th commandment: never underestimate the stress the learner is under when trying to communicate in the target language (Ricci Garotti [2009: 13] draws a parallel with the novice dancer's fear of missing a step and looking a fool in public). Speaking a foreign language involves risk, and therefore creates anxiety. A certain amount of anxiety, sometimes called *facilitating anxiety*, can focus the mind and actually improve L2 performance, but excessive strain, or *debilitating anxiety*, inhibits learners and prevents them from displaying their true communicative ability. In educational contexts, anxiety needs to be taken into account in evaluating learners' performance.

Of more practical use than the 'ten commandments' is the framework for motivational strategies that Dörnyei outlines (2001: 119-137) to advise teachers on how to maximise outcomes during the various phases of the Process Model described in chapter 3. This involves four stages: (i) creating the basic motivational conditions; (ii) generating student motivation; (iii) maintaining and protecting motivation; (iv) encouraging positive self-evaluation.

For stage 1, the most important element in creating the basic motivational conditions is the teacher herself. Apart from the obvious qualities of competence in the target language, employment of an appropriate methodology for the age and level of the students, and treating all learners equally, another factor that can have great impact on motivation is whether she displays enthusiasm (it is no coincidence that the noun *enthusiasm* is often premodified by the adjective *infectious*). Of course, for the teacher to be enthusiastic she must herself be motivated, and it is a regrettable fact (dealt with later in this chapter) that language teachers in many educational contexts are demotivated.

Other factors that Dörnyei considers relevant to stage 1 are the establishment of a pleasant and supportive atmosphere in the classroom, something which may depend upon the institution as a whole and not just the individual teacher, and the creation of a cohesive learner group with appropriate group norms. This second point again necessitates flexibility at institutional level: bad chemistry between individual learners may require changing the composition of classes, even at the cost of creating imbalances of a more manageable nature (it is better to move a student to a class in which the level is slightly too high rather than leave him in a group with someone he clearly loathes). Some teachers like to adopt a hands-on approach from the beginning, encouraging the learners to discuss and agree upon a set of class rules that all will (promise to) abide by. It is important to foster a sense of solidarity within the group; like all teachers with decades of experience, I have in my time encountered students who were extremely uncooperative, others who exhibited the telltale signs of cocaine abuse, a few who stuck me as being certifiably insane and two or three who were not too fussy about personal hygiene, but in most cases the rest of the class were sufficiently united to marginalise the difficult individual and carry on with their endeavours to learn English.

Stage 2, generating student motivation, corresponds to the preactional phase of the process model. The teacher's aims during this stage are to enhance the learners' language-related values and attitudes (e.g. encouraging instrumental motivation by making them aware of the practical benefits of acquiring the target language, or fostering integrative motivation by exposing learners to aspects of the L2 culture), increasing the learners' goal-orientedness (e.g. helping them to set realisable personal goals), making the curriculum and activities relevant to the learners' level and needs, and creating realistic learner beliefs (e.g. by inviting feedback, providing encouragement but also working 'to sort out some of the most far-fetched expectations and get rid of the preconceived notions and prejudices that are likely to hinder L2 attainment' [*Ibid.*: 126]).

The next stage, maintaining and protecting motivation, corresponds to the actional phase of the process model. To reinforce the learners' actions, the teacher's tasks include helping them motivate themselves through the setting of short- and midterm goals, maintaining the intrinsic enjoyment of the learning experience with the judicious choice of activities and tasks, and protecting the learners' self-image within the group context (e.g. by displaying prudence and sensitivity over such matters as error correction or asking individuals to engage in "risky" L2 activities that could potentially expose them to public failure). As we saw in the Cagliari case study, good learners are autonomous learners with a healthy degree of self-confidence. To boost self-confidence, a few words of encouragement are always useful but in themselves are not enough. The choice of activities is important: if the learners do nothing but exercises designed to "catch them out", or expose what they don't know or can't do, their learning experience is one of being constantly reminded of their deficiencies; if, on the other hand, they engage in activities that give them an opportunity to show what they *can* do, the experience of achieving something meaningful is likely to enhance their self-confidence. Learner autonomy can also be developed through the choice of tasks and activities.

Students should not be spoon-fed or permitted to remain passive absorbers rather that active foragers; instead, they should be set tasks that oblige them to seek information (the internet can be a wonderful resource if used judiciously), cooperate with fellow learners and play an active role in the learning process.

Self-confidence and autonomy should lead to self-motivation. Self-motivated learners take control of and assume responsibility for the various factors involved in striving to achieve their goal: their emotions, their response to practical difficulties and logistical obstacles, dealing with the interference of competing goals, and adopting appropriate learning strategies both inside and outside the classroom. And if they are truly self-motivated, like F in the Cagliari case study, they will also accept responsibility for unsatisfactory outcomes and take the necessary action to rectify the situation.

Finally, stage 4 corresponds to the postactional phase of retrospective self-evaluation. Here the teacher has an opportunity to provide motivational feedback that pinpoints positive achievements but is nevertheless honest (a poor test score is a poor test score and it insults the learner's intelligence to pretend otherwise). Attributing unsatisfactory results to the eminently reversible cause of insufficient effort enables learners to maintain faith in their essential ability. The aim is to maximise the learners' satisfaction and thus encourage them to continue to work towards their language goal. Satisfied students help to create a pleasant atmosphere in the classroom and contribute to the cohesiveness of the group (stage 1 features), which means that the framework for motivational strategies functions like a virtuous circle that parallels the cyclic nature of the process model.

From the teacher's point of view, it is an advantage if the testing and evaluation of achievement is carried out by a third party, such as a GCE A'level board in the UK or an international language testing organisation like Cambridge ESOL. In these circumstances the teacher's attempts to be supportive and encouraging do not conflict with her role as examination designer and rater. In some contexts, particularly at university level, teachers are also examiners, which may mean that all their efforts during the year to gain the learners' trust risk being undermined when the exam results are published. The people who teach general English to the students investigated in the Cagliari survey are in that invidious situation. Furthermore, after publication of the results, the students have a right to see their papers, which is an opportunity for them to identify the specific areas of their lexicogrammatical competence that require improvement, but is an occasion that can also degenerate into "plea bargaining", tearful appeals for clemency or accusations that the teacher/examiner has not treated all candidates equally. To counter such allegations, the teachers concerned design tests that entail objective marking that leaves very little scope for interpretation. They consist mostly of discrete point testing rather than a global assessment of communicative skills, and are therefore not the sort of examinations that permit learners to express themselves in the target language and show what they can really do. The constraints of the institutional context oblige teachers to do things that not only go against the professional grain, but are also not conducive to reinforcing learners' motivation.

Good scores in tests do not always have a positive effect on learners' motivation since they may deflect attention from the original goal of learning the L2; goal-orientedness mutates into grade-orientedness, and the worthy aim of learning to communicate effectively in a second language is replaced by a fixation with obtaining certification that may or may not give an accurate picture of one's communicative competence. For the truly motivated language learner, a positive self-assessment of achievement provides more satisfaction that the extrinsic reward of an examination grade.

L2 motivation is improved if we have the opportunity to study the language in a way that suits our personal cognitive and learning styles. Dörnyei and Skehan (2003: 602) make an admirably concise distinction between the two: 'The former can be defined as a predisposition to process information in a characteristic manner while the latter can be defined as a typical preference for approaching learning in general'. As regards cognitive styles, psychologists often distinguish between field-dependent (FD) people, who tend to perceive a wood, and field-independent (FI) people, who see a collection of individual trees. FD people tend to have global and sometimes impulsive preferences in learning, while FI people favour an analytic, reflective approach. Other differences in learning styles lead us to distinguish between visual learners, who like reading or studying charts and tables, auditory learners, who respond better to lectures and seminars, and tactile/kinesthetic learners, who prefer a hands-on, learning-by-doing approach. Many language schools and university departments give newly enrolled students a learning-styles diagnostic test to help them understand themselves better and thus, it is hoped, choose appropriate activities and learning strategies. If a teacher has twenty students in a class, it is likely that several different learning styles will be represented, so it is obvious that she cannot please all the learners all the time. By setting up a wide variety of activities, however, she will probably do something that is just right for each individual at some time or other.

And we are back to the teacher, the person who has a key role in generating and maintaining learners' motivation. As mentioned earlier, if teachers are to motivate their students, it helps if they are motivated themselves. This is frequently not the case.

In many countries, teachers of all disciplines are poorly paid. One line of thinking is that this is a good thing because society wants its teachers, like its priests, to have a vocation, or a calling, rather than material ambitions, and it is true that many young teachers start out with very high intrinsic motivation because they derive a great sense of fulfilment from working with young people and observing their progress. But young teachers grow older, have children of their own and, not surprisingly, begin to weary of the double-think that states that to attract the best bankers we must offer enormous salaries and bonuses, but to get the most committed teachers we must do precisely the opposite. The temporal dimension is as important in teachers' motivation as it is in learners' motivation, and far too often the trend is negative.

Other factors that can demotivate teachers include stress, a lack of opportunities for career advancement, ministerial or institutional impositions that reduce their efficacy in the classroom, low social and professional status, and – for those in state schools – resentment at being blamed for the high rates of juvenile delinquency, teenage pregnancy and many other ills in society.

Despite all this, truly inspirational teachers continue to emerge and, astonishingly, maintain a certain zest throughout their careers. They ignite learners' motivation with their enthusiasm, then sustain it with their professional competence. It is a symbiotic relationship, however, for the achievements of those learners gives the teachers satisfaction, and satisfaction nourishes renewed motivation.

Afterword

While we await a miracle method that really works, or the discovery of a way to activate the brain's capacity for extraordinary language acquisition, we must reconcile ourselves to the fact that for most of us learning a foreign language requires a lot of effort and a lot of time. Motivating ourselves to make that kind of investment entails coordinating and directing our cognitive, psychological and affective resources. To convince ourselves that the endeavour is worth persevering with, it is a good idea to remind ourselves from time to time of what we stand to gain if we achieve our goal. This work began with three quotations on motivation, so it is perhaps fitting to conclude with three quotations on the benefits of knowing another language:

As a hawk flieth not high with one wing, even so a man reacheth not to excellence with one tongue.
Roger Ascham, tutor to Queen Elizabeth I

Those who know nothing of a foreign language know nothing of their own.
Goethe

To have another language is to possess a second soul.
Charlemagne

Appendix 1

Cagliari Survey: Questionnaire 1 (October 2008)

Please indicate your reaction to the following statements.
Option A = I strongly agree
Option B = I agree
Option C = I partially agree
Option D = I partially disagree
Option E = I disagree
Option F = I strongly disagree

1. For me studying English is an enjoyable intellectual activity.

   A ☐   B ☐   C ☐   D ☐   E ☐   F ☐

2. I like the sound of the English language.

   A ☐   B ☐   C ☐   D ☐   E ☐   F ☐

3. Studying English grammar is boring.

   A ☐   B ☐   C ☐   D ☐   E ☐   F ☐

4. Even if I were not studying at university, I would try to improve my English.

   A ☐   B ☐   C ☐   D ☐   E ☐   F ☐

5. Sometimes I get fed up with studying English.

   A ☐   B ☐   C ☐   D ☐   E ☐   F ☐

Appendix 1

6. For me it is more important to be able to communicate effectively in English than to get good grades in the exams.

   A □   B □   C □   D □   E □   F □

7. My main reason for choosing to study English is to improve my chances of finding a good job.

   A □   B □   C □   D □   E □   F □

8. In an ideal situation, I would study another language rather than English.

   A □   B □   C □   D □   E □   F □

9. When I study English I focus only on what I need to pass the exam.

   A □   B □   C □   D □   E □   F □

10. I am obliged to study English because nowadays you can't do without this language.

    A □   B □   C □   D □   E □   F □

11. I will have more chance of earning a good salary if I manage to reach a high level of competence in English.

    A □   B □   C □   D □   E □   F □

12. For me passing the exams of English is more important than my real communicative ability in the language.

    A ☐   B ☐   C ☐   D ☐   E ☐   F ☐

PERSONAL DETAILS

Age: 18-20 ☐   21-25 ☐   26+ ☐
Sex: Male ☐   Female ☐
Current level of English:
Elementary ☐   Pre-intermediate ☐   Intermediate or above ☐
Degree course: Lcom ☐   Lcult ☐   Lmed ☐

Thankyou for your cooperation.

Source: Buckledee (2008)

Appendix 2

Cagliari Survey: Questionnaire 2 (May/June 2009)

1. Since the beginning of the academic year your desire to learn English has:

A. ☐ increased considerably
B. ☐ increased somewhat
C. ☐ remained unchanged
D. ☐ diminished somewhat
E. ☐ diminished considerably

2. Are you satisfied with the progress you've made in English over the last seven or eight months?

A. ☐ really satisfied
B. ☐ fairly satisfied
C. ☐ neither satisfied nor dissatisfied
D. ☐ somewhat dissatisfied
E. ☐ extremely dissatisfied

3. As regards the subject of English language (and only English language), give a mark between 5 (excellent) and 1 (very poor). Don't worry. This questionnaire is anonymous.

a. ____ The teaching
b. ____ The organisation of timetables and syllabi
c. ____ The relevance of the degree course to the world of work

Appendix 2

PERSONAL DETAILS
Age: 18-20 □   21-25 □   26+ □
Sex: Male □   Female □
Current level of English:
Post-Elementary □ Preintermediate □ Intermediate or higher □
Degree course: Lcom □   Lcult □   Lmed □

Thankyou for your cooperation.

Source: Buckledee (2009)

Appendix 3

Cagliari Survey: Questionnaire 3 (3 and 22 June 2010)

1. Since you enrolled on your degree course, your desire to learn English has:

A. ☐ increased considerably
B. ☐ increased somewhat
C. ☐ remained unchanged
D. ☐ diminished somewhat
E. ☐ diminished considerably

2. Are you satisfied with the progress you've made in English over the last 20 months?

A. ☐ really satisfied
B. ☐ fairly satisfied
C. ☐ neither satisfied nor dissatisfied
D. ☐ somewhat dissatisfied
E. ☐ extremely dissatisfied

If for question 2 you indicated A, B or C please answer question 3.

If for question 2 you indicated D, E o F please answer question 4.

Appendix 3

3. To what factors do you attribute your (relatively) good progress in English?

A. ☐ Your own ability and/or other personal qualities (intelligence, powers of concentration etc.)
B. ☐ Your capacity to study and learn despite certain practical difficulties
C. ☐ Self-motivation and/or your ability to realise personal goals
D. ☐ Other reasons (please specify): _____

4. To what factors do you attribute your (relatively) disappointing progress in English?

A. ☐ Insufficient effort or other temporary shortcomings
B. ☐ The distraction of personal problems or practical difficulties (timetable, travelling etc.)
C. ☐ No aptitude for studying languages or the English language in particular
D. ☐ Other reasons (please specify): _____

PERSONAL DETAILS

Age: 19-21 ☐   22-26 ☐   27+ ☐
Sex: Male ☐   Female ☐
Level of English when you enrolled:
Elementare ☐ Preintermedio+ ☐ Intermedio+ ☐
Degree course: Lcom ☐   Lcult ☐   Lmed ☐

Source: Buckledee (in press)

Appendix 4

Cagliari Survey – questionnaire 4 (June 2011)

1. Indicate the sentence that best represents how you see yourself.

A. ☐ I would like to become really good at English and I think I'm on the way to achieving that objective.
B. ☐ I would like to become really good at English but I don't think I'm making the progress necessary to make my wish come true.
C. ☐ I don't expect to become really good at English. I know my limits.

2. Indicate the sentence that best represents your point of view.

A. ☐ I think studying a foreign language should be enjoyable. If I get bored I stop studying.
B. ☐ Because of my parents I feel I have a duty to study English properly even when I don't really feel like it.
C. ☐ I study English willingly. Sometimes it's hard work but it's rewarding all the same.

3. Up to now your experiences of studying English at school and/or university have been:

A. ☐ definitely positive
B. ☐ more positive than negative
C. ☐ more negative than positive
D. ☐ definitely negative

Appendix 4

4. Which sentence describes you best?

A. ☐ I know how to study English. I use various learning strategies and I am able to organise my time.
B. ☐ I think I'm capable of reaching a good level of English but I need advice on how to study effectively.
C. ☐ It isn't a question of methods or strategies. I'm just not really cut out for learning English.

PERSONAL DETAILS
Age: 20-22 ☐   23-27 ☐   28+ ☐
Sex: Male ☐   Female ☐
Level of English when you enrolled at the Faculty:
Elementary ☐   Preintermediate ☐ Intermediate+ ☐
Degree course: Lcom ☐   Lcult ☐   Lmed ☐

References

Allport, G.W. (1958), *The Nature of Prejudice*, New York: Doubleday

Bacon, S. and Finnemann, M. (1992), 'Sex differences in self-reported beliefs about foreign-language learning and authentic oral and input', *Language Learning* 42: 471-495

Baker, C. (1988), *Key Issues in Bilingualism and Bilingual Education*, Cleveland, Avon (UK): Multilingual Matters

Baker, S.C. and MacIntyre, P.D. (2003), 'The Role of Gender and Immersion in Communication and Second Language Orientations', in Dörnyei (ed), pp 65-96

Bandura, A. (1993), 'Perceived self-efficacy in cognitive development and functioning', *Educational Psychologist*, 28: 117-148

Brown, J.D. (2001), *Using Surveys in Language Programs*, Cambridge: Cambridge University Press

Buckledee, S. (2008), 'Motivation and Second Language Acquisition' in Komar and Mozetič, pp 159-170

Buckledee, S. (2009), 'Motivation and Second Language Acquisition: Phase 2 of a Longitudinal Study of Undergraduate Students at an Italian University', in *Letterature Straniere &*, 12: 23-33

Buckledee, S. (in press), 'Atttribution Theory and Language Learners' Maintenance or Loss of Motivation: phase 3 of a longitudinal study of undergraduate students at an Italian university'

Burstall, C. (1975), 'Factors affecting foreign-language learning: a consideration of some relevant research findings', *Language Teaching and Linguistics Abstracts* 8: 105-125

Chomsky, N. (1976), *Reflections on language*, London: Temple Smith

Clément, R. (1980), 'Ethnicity, contact and communicative competence in a second language', in Giles *at al* (eds), pp 147-154

Clément, R., Dörnyei, Z., and Noels, K.A. (1994), 'Motivation, self-confidence and group cohesion in the foreign language classroom', *Language Learning*, 44: 417-448

Cook, V. (2001), *Second Language Learning and Teaching*, London: Hodder Arnold

Cortazzi, M., Hall, B. and Rafik Galea, S. (eds) [1996], *Proceedings of the Research Students' Conference*, Leicester: University of Leicester

Covington, M. (1992), *Making the grade: A self-worth perspective on motivation and school reform*, Cambridge: Cambridge University Press

Csizer, K. and Dörnyei, Z. (2005), 'Language learners' motivational profiles and their motivated learning behaviour', *Language Learning*, 55: 613-659

Deci, E.L. and Ryan, R.M. (1985), *Intrinsic motivation and self-determination in human behavior*, New York: Plenum

Dörnyei, Z. (2001), *Teaching and Researching Motivation*, Harlow (UK): Pearson Education Limited

Dörnyei, Z. (2003a), *Questionnaires in Second Language Research*, New Jersey: Lawrence Erlbaum Associates

Dörnyei, Z. (ed) [2003b], *Attitudes, Orientations, and Motivations in Language Learning*, Oxford: Blackwell Publishing

Dörnyei, Z. (2005), *The Psychology of the Language Learner: Individual Differences in Second Language Acquisition*, Mahwah (NJ), USA: Lawrence Erlbaum

Dörnyei, Z. and Csizér, K. (1998), 'Ten commandments for motivating language learners: Results of an empirical study', *Language Teaching Research*, 2: 203-229

Dörnyei, Z. and Ottó, I. (1998), 'Motivation in action: A process model of L2 motivation', *Working Papers in Applied Linguistics* (Thames Valley University, London), 4: 43-69

Dörnyei, Z. and Skehan, P. (2003), 'Individual Differences in L2 Learning', in Doughty and Long, pp 589-630

Dörnyei, Z. and Schmidt, R. (eds) [2001], *Motivation and Second Language Acquisition*, Honolulu: University of Hawai'I Press

Dörnyei, Z. and Csizér, K. (2005), 'The Effects of Interpercultural Contact and Tourism on Language Attitudes and Language Learning Motivation', *Journal of Language and Social Psychology*, 24: 327-357

Doughty, C.J. and Long, M.H. (eds) [2003], *The Handbook of Second Language Acquisition*, Oxford: Blackwell Publishing

Efklides, A., Kuhl, J. and Sorrentino, R.M. (eds) [2010], *Trends and Prospects in Motivation Research*, Dordrecht (The Netherlands): Kluver Academic Publishers

Ellis, R. (2008²), *The Study of Second Language Acquisition*, Oxford: Oxford University Press

Gardner, R.C. (1985a), *The Attitude/Motivation Test Battery: Technical Report*, London (Canada): University of Western Ontario

Gardner, R.C. (1985b), *Social Psychology and Second Language Learning: The Role of Attitude and Motivation*, London: Edward Arnold

Gardner, R.C. (2001), 'Integrative Motivation and Second Language Acquisition', in Dörnyei and Schmidt, pp 1-19

Gardner, R.C. and MacIntyre, P.D. (1993), 'A student's contribution to second language learning. Part 1: Cognitive variables', *Language Teaching* 25/4: 211-220

Gardner, R.C. and Lambert, W. (1972), *Attitudes and Motivation in Second Language Learning*, Rowley (Mass.): Newbury House

Giles, H., Robinson, W.P. and Smith, P.M. (eds) [1980], *Language: Social Pschological Perspectives*, Oxford: Pergamon

Gollwitzer, P.M. and Bargh, J.A. (eds) [1986], *The psychology of action: Linking cognition and motivation to behaviour*, New York: Guilford Press

Halliday, M.A.K., Teubert, W., Yallop, C. and Cermáková, A. (2004), *Lexicology and Corpus Linguistics*, London and New York: continuum

Halish, F. and Kuhl, J. (eds) [1987], *Motivation, intention and volition*, Berlin: Springer

Higgins, E.T. (1989), 'Self-discrepancy: A theory relating self and affect', *Psychological Review*, 94: 319-340

Komar, S. and and Mozetič, U. (eds) [2008], *As You Write It: Issues in Literature, Language and Translation in the Context of Europe in the 21st Century*, Ljubljana (Slovenia): Slovensko društvo za angleške študijei

Kuhl, J. (1987), 'Action control: The maintenance of motivational states', in Halish and Kuhl (eds), pp 279-291

Lenneberg, E. (1967), *Biological Foundations of Language*, New York: John Wiley

Little, D., Ridley, J. and Ushioda, E. (eds) [2003], *Learner Autonomy in the Foreign Language Classroom: Teacher, Learner, Curriculum, Assessment*, Dublin: Authentik

Locke, E.A. and Latham, G.P. (1990), *A theory of goal setting and task performance*, Englewood Cliffs, NJ, USA: Prentice Hall

Ludwig, J. (1983), 'Attitudes and expectations: a profile of female and male students of college French, German and Spanish', *The Modern Language Journal* 67: 216-227

MacIntyre, P.D., Clément, R., Dörnyei, Z. and Noels, K. (1998), 'Conceptualizing Willingness to Communicate in a L2: A Situated Model of Confidence and Affiliation', *Modern Language Journal*, 82: 547

MacIntyre, P.D., Baker, S.C., Clément, R. and Donovan, L.A. (2003), 'Sex and Age Effects on Willingness to Communicate, Anxiety, Perceived Competence, and L2 Motivation Among Junior High School French Immersion Students', in Dörnyei (ed), pp 137-165

Noels, K.A., Pelletier, L.G., Clément, R. and Vallerand, R.J. (2003), 'Why Are You Learning a Second Language? Motivational Orientations and Self-Determination Theory', in Dörnyei (ed), pp 33-63

Oller, J. and Perkins, K. (1978), 'Intelligence and language proficiency as sources of variance in self-reported affective variables', *Language Learning*, 28: 85-97

Pintrich, P.R. and Schunk, D.H. (1996), *Motivation in education: Theory, research and applications*, Englewood Cliffs, NJ, USA: Prentice Hall

Prabhu, N.S. (1987), *Second Language Pedagogy*, Oxford: Oxford University Press

Ricci Garotti, F. (2009), 'Di demotivazione si può guarire', *Scuola e Lingue Moderne*, 1-3: 10-15

Schumann, J. (1998), *The neurobiology of affect in language*, Oxford: Blackwell Publishing

Schumann, J. (2001), 'Learning as Foraging', in Dörnyei and Schmidt (eds), pp 21-28

Skehan, P. (1989), *Individual Differences in Second Language Learning*, London: Edward Arnold

Sorrentino, R.M. (1996), 'The role of conscious thought in a theory of motivation and cognition: The uncertainty orientation paradigm', in Gollwitzer *et al*, pp 619-614

Sorrentino, R.M., Walker, A.M., Hodson, G. and Roney, Ch.J.R. (2010). 'A theory of uncertainty motivation: The interplay of motivation, cognition and affect', in Efklides *et al*, pp 187-206

Spivak, D.L. (1989), *Kak stat' polyglotom* (How one becomes a polyglot), St Petersburg: privately published

Spolsky, B. (1989), *Conditions for Second Language Learning*, Oxford: Oxford University Press

Syed, Z. (2001), 'Notions of Self in Foreign Language Learning: a Qualitative Analysis', in Dörnyei and Schmidt (eds), pp 127-148

Teubert, W. and Cermáková, A. (2004), 'Directions in corpus linguistics', in Halliday *et al*

Thornton, B. (1996), 'Attitudes to Foreign Languages: A Preliminary Report', in Cortazzi *et al*

Tremblay, P.F. and Gardner, R.C. (1995), 'Expanding the motivation construct in language learning', *Modern Language Journal*, 79: 505-520

Tremblay, P.F., Goldberg, M.P. and Gardner, R.C. (1995), 'Trait and state motivation and the acquisition of Hebrew vocabulary', *Canadian Journal of Behavioural Science*, 27: 356-370

Ushioda, E. (2003), 'Motivation as a socially mediated process', in Little *et al* (eds)

Ushioda, E. (2001), 'Language Learning at University: Exploring the Role of Motivational Thinking', in Dörnyei and Schmidt (eds), pp 93-125

Weiner, B. (1986), *An attributional theory of motivation and emotion*, New York: Springer-Verlag

Weiner, B. (1992), *Human motivation: Metaphors, theories and research*, Newbury Park (CA), USA: Sage

Williams, M., Burden, R.L. and Al-Baharna, S. (2001), 'Making Sense of Success and Failure: The role of the individual in motivation theory', in Dörnyei and Schmidt, pp 171-184

Willis. J. (1996), *A framework for task-based learning*, Harlow (UK): Longman

Worrall, N. and Tsarna, H. (1987), 'Influences on learner attitudes towards foreign language and culture', *Educational Research*, 41: 197-208

Index

acquisition vs learning 31, 140, 144

action control 47, 65, 75, 102, 108, 112, 136

actional outcome 66

actional phase 61, 64-66, 68, 75, 84, 102, 108, 131, 132, 153

actual self 104, 113, 124, 129, 133, 137

Allport, G.W. 16

AMBT (Attitude/Motivation Test Battery) 11, 14, 35, 142

amotivation 42

anxiety 28, 37, 46, 141, 142, 146, 147, 150

appraisal of learning situation 47, 61, 64, 69, 75, 83, 86, 102, 107, 112, 113, 135, 136

aptitude 6, 11, 23, 28, 137

attitudes 11-17, 148

attitudes toward the learning situation 30-38

attribution(s) 62, 66, 67, 89-92, 101-105, 108, 114-116, 131, 138, 154

autonomy 42, 65, 84, 105, 111, 112, 122, 125, 132, 137, 153

Bacon, S. 144

Baker, C. 13

Baker, S.C. 146, 147

Bandura, A. 41

Broca's area 21

Brown, J.D. 51, 57

Buckledee, S. 48, 49, 71, 79, 96

Burstall, C. 144

Cermáková, A. 16

Chomsky, N. 140

Clément, R. 27, 33, 41

cognitive styles 156, 157

Contact theory 16

Cook, V. 15, 17

Covington, M. 41

critical period hypothesis 140, 141

Csizér, K. 16, 104, 113, 149, 150

Index

Deci, E.L. 42

Dörnyei, Z. 10, 12, 16, 18, 19, 20, 27, 33, 38, 47, 51, 57, 60, 61-68, 84, 88, 89, 104, 113, 131, 149, 150, 151, 156

Ellis, R. 17, 23, 144, 145

expectancy-value theories 40-41, 63, 68, 101

extrinsic motivation 27, 44, 105

Finnemann, M. 144

foraging 43-45, 105, 108

foreign language vs second language 33, 147

Gardner, R.C. 11, 13, 18, 23, 27-38, 143, 144

goal orientations 39, 63, 152

goal-setting theory 39-40, 102

goal theories 30, 38-39, 62

heritage language 117, 119

Higgins, E.T. 104, 113

hyperpolyglot 21, 24

ideal language self 104, 113, 124, 126, 129, 132, 137

ideal self 104, 113

identity and language 15, 26, 119

instrumental motivation 27-38, 41, 48-59, 85, 144, 145, 148, 153

integrative motivation 27-38, 41, 86, 104, 147, 150, 152

integrativeness 30-38, 41, 61, 68, 106

intention
  formation 62-64, 131
  enactment 64-66, 131

internal standards 67

intrinsic motivation 27, 41, 48-59, 63, 86, 134, 149

Kenrick, D. 21

Krebs, E. 21

Kuhl, J. 63

Kus, M. 24

Lambert, W. 27, 144

Latham, G.P. 39, 102, 141

Law of Seven 22

learning styles 156, 157

Lenneberg, E. 140

Linguistic Minorities Report 15

linguistic self-confidence 33, 41, 46, 63, 67, 87, 112, 113, 153

Locke, E.A. 39, 102, 141

Ludwig, J. 145

Machiavellian motivation 35

MacIntyre, P.D. 23, 46, 141-143, 146, 147

Mezzofanti, G. 21

motivation

conscious/unconscious 19, 20

definition of 17-20

neurobiology 43, 61, 68, 113

Noels, K.A. 33, 41, 42

Oller, J. 35

orientations 30, 39, 61, 148

action orientation 63, 68

state orientation 63, 68

Ottó, I. 19, 61-68, 84, 131

ought self 104

Perkins, K. 35

Pintrich, P.R. 39

polyglot(tism) 21, 22

postactional phase 61, 66-67, 87, 88, 113, 154

Prabhu, N.S. 48

preactional phase 61-64, 68, 84, 131, 152

process model 61-68, 84, 88, 108, 114, 131, 151, 152

Pygmalion 22

Resultative Motivation Hypothesis 56

Ricci Garotti, F. 150

Ryan, R.M. 42

Schumann, J. 43, 44, 45, 61, 65, 113

Schunk, D.H. 39

self-determination theory 41-42, 58, 63, 64, 65, 68, 86, 113

self-discrepancy theory 104

self-efficacy theory 41, 63, 67, 113

self-regulation 84, 102, 108, 112, 113, 116, 122, 130, 132, 137

self-worth theory 41, 61, 63, 67, 87, 113

Shaw, G.B. 22

Skehan, P. 10, 20, 27, 38, 56, 60, 156

Smythe, P. 27

Socio-educational model 28-38

Index

Sorrentino, R.M. 19, 20
Spivak, D.L. 22
Spolsky, B. 144
state motivation 47
stimulus appraisal 44
Syed, Z. 117

task-based learning 48
task motivation 47
Teubert, W. 16
Thornton, B. 14, 15
trait motivation 47
Tremblay, P.F. 33, 47
Tsarna, H. 144, 146

Universal Grammar 140, 141
Ushioda, E. 90, 101, 114, 115, 116

Weiner, B. 89, 100
Williams, M. 91, 101
willingness to communicate (WTC) 46-47, 141, 142, 146, 148
Willis. J. 48
Wolfson, L. 23, 24
Worrall, N. 144, 146